T0069760

WHAT THE AMISH TEACH US

PLAIN LIVING IN A BUSY WORLD

WHAT

THE

AMISH

TEACH

US

Donald B. Kraybill

Johns Hopkins University Press | BALTIMORE

© 2021 Johns Hopkins University Press
All rights reserved. Published 2021
Printed in the United States of America on acid-free paper
2 4 6 8 9 7 5 3

Johns Hopkins University Press
2715 North Charles Street
Baltimore, Maryland 21218-4363
www.press.jhu.edu

Library of Congress Cataloging-in-Publication Data

Names: Kraybill, Donald B., author.
Title: What the Amish teach us : plain living in a busy world / Donald B. Kraybill.
Description: Baltimore : Johns Hopkins University Press, 2021. | Includes
bibliographical references and index.
Identifiers: LCCN 2020057352 | ISBN 9781421442174 (hardcover) |
ISBN 9781421442181 (ebook)
Subjects: LCSH: Conduct of life. | Amish—Conduct of life.
Classification: LCC BJ1589 K73 2021 | DDC 158.1—dc23
LC record available at https://lccn.loc.gov/2020057352

A catalog record for this book is available from the British Library.

Special discounts are available for bulk purchases of this book. For more information,
please contact Special Sales at specialsales@jh.edu.

CONTENTS

When Old Is New Again

I know it sounds audacious. But it's true. The Amish have much to teach us. It may seem strange, even surreal, to turn to one of America's most traditional groups for lessons about living in a hyper-tech world— especially a horse-driving people who have resisted "progress" by snubbing cars, public grid power, and even high school education.

Nonetheless, the Amish deserve a hearing. Their wisdom confirms that old turns new again. Or in the words of another truism, perhaps they're so far be-hind, they're out ahead. So before you toss aside this seemingly ludicrous notion that we can learn some-thing from a low-tech people, consider these facts.

The Amish have out-Ubered Uber since they began hiring rides from neighbors nearly a century ago. They were also into solar power before it was green. Their "engineers" have developed sophisticated sky tubes for lighting off-grid buildings. Amish entrepreneurs, who never entered high school, have built thousands of successful businesses. Moreover, Amish collaboration with scientists in advanced genomic research has brought pathbreaking medical discoveries. The loneliness epidemic that stalks our society has largely bypassed Amishland. And these are the people whose courage enabled them to forgive, within hours, the man who gunned down ten of their children. They have much to teach us.

Amish ways intrigue. The so-called reality TV shows *Breaking Amish* and *Amish Mafia* capture high viewer ratings. The odd genre of "bonnet novels," which have flooded bookshelves over the past two decades, has made millions in sales. Amish-wannabe books like *Almost Amish: One Woman's Quest for a Slower, Simpler, More Sustainable Life* also abound. Amish quilts continue to enchant the world of modern art. Plus, some twenty million tourists generate $2 billion a year for a peek at Amish life in Pennsylvania and the Midwest. On many a metric, the Amish score high.

Yet beneath our curiosity, we hold widely different views of these traditional people.

Some of us applaud their strong families, staunch communities, and stubborn resistance to advanced technology. These untarnished tillers of the soil—a kind of eighteenth-century culture plopped into twenty-first-century life—appear to preserve the best of what we used to be, a kind of utopian remnant of a virtuous American past. Champions of this blissful view consider America's Amish the guardians of an ethical tradition that still sets a standard for today.

Others see the Amish as vestiges of a bygone era—a cute relic of colonial life, stirring apple butter over a fire, churning milk by hand, and baking bread in a beehive oven—who have nothing to offer us now.

Still other people deride them—claiming that Amish society stifles individual freedom and hampers human creativity. These critics consider the Amish an archaic group that perpetuates patriarchy, in-group marriage, and taboos on divorce. They allege that Amish members blindly follow communal traditions that restrict education, reject science, and shun many achievements of the twentieth century.

The real Amish, in all their diversity, are not so easy to pin down.

Discontent with modern life leads some people to fantasize that the Amish can save us or at least lead us out of our cultural quagmire. For example, the 2017 post-apocalyptic novel *When the English Fall* depicts Amish people as low-tech organic farmers who survive the collapse of American civilization as it implodes into anarchy from climate change. Frankly, I don't think the Amish can save us. And they would be quick to agree. Still—the thought intrigues.

Overwhelmed with the troubles of our times or the troubles in their own lives, some seekers see a lot of good in the Amish—so much so that they yearn to join them. However, I'm not recruiting for the Amish. I'm not even hinting that you should join an Amish community or pack your bags and head for the boondocks. Nor am I proposing that we cut and paste their habits into our contemporary lives and try to mimic how they live. You may want to explore some of those options, but that's not what this book's about.

So what *is* this book about?

I have given hundreds of presentations on Amish culture as a scholar of Anabaptist groups and culture. After these presentations, people often ask, "So what did you learn from the Amish?" This book answers that question. It chronicles the lessons they have taught me, lessons of benefit for all of us that include universal themes of family and community.

For me, Amish ways disturb and disrupt. They disturb some assumptions that I take for granted. They disrupt my old habits, my predispositions, and my fixed understandings of how I think the world works. They certainly uproot my a priori assumptions about progress and prod me to question why I do what I do. In this sense, the Amish are silent social critics—offering a critique of modern culture that is intellectually provocative yet always practical.

An excursion into Amish life sheds light on our culture and allows us to see our own lives from a new perspective. Understanding how they cope with modernity invites us to examine our own assumptions and practices more carefully. It also nudges us to reflect more deeply on the meaning of our lives.

Amish life is not an antidote for all our modern ills. The Amish are not perfect or angelic. As one grandmother told me, "We have our good ones and our bad ones just like you." Like any society, they have shortcomings and social maladies aplenty. Despite those warts, they have much to teach us.

Amish people did not invent all their folkways. Many are residuals of early twentieth-century rural life. Their view of government and urban life, their use of one-room schools, and their mutual aid activities, such as barn raisings, hang on from earlier days. Some habits, like forgiveness, carry a distinctive Amish trademark. Yet even that custom appears in many other religions, as well as in the practice of psychotherapy.

Meanwhile, the Amish thrive. Predictions in the 1950s of their imminent demise were dead wrong. Doubling every twenty years, their population of 360,000 lives in six hundred settlements across thirty-one states and four Canadian provinces. Even so, they're but a speck among the 365 million who live in the United States and Canada.

Amish and Mennonites, another Christian group, share roots that reach back to the Anabaptist movement, which began in Switzerland in 1525. A simple but provocative question sparked the beginning of their Radical Reformation: Does the church or the state have authority to regulate baptism? The adult-baptizing Anabaptists, who refused to christen infants, insisted that church and scripture held sole authority over baptism. This heretical idea—of the separation of church and state—triggered widespread persecution and martyrdom of Anabaptists.

Over a century and a half later, the Swiss Anabaptists separated into the Amish and Mennonite branches in 1693. Before and after this division, some of the Anabaptist groups fleeing oppression immigrated to North America. By then, the painful persecution in their history had galvanized in Amish minds a strong separatist stance, which persists today. Their religious principle of *separation from the world* involves symbolic clothing, horse-drawn transportation, and the absence of church buildings, among many other things. "The Amish have been social distancing from the world for a long time," quipped one person amid the COVID-19 pandemic.

✣

The essays in this book emerged from conversations with hundreds of Amish people, from thousands of hours of fieldwork in different states, and from my ruminations over four decades of research. This col-

lection is not a comprehensive or balanced introduc-
tion to Amish life. From a plethora of possible themes,
I selected twenty-two that I find most provocative,
ones that have reshaped my thinking and given me
new insights for living in a hyper-everything world.

I refer to "the Amish" as if all their forty affiliations
(subgroups) can be consolidated in a single group of
like-dressing, same-believing people. Lumping them
into one culture, however, overlooks their diversity,
because each affiliation has its distinctive way of life—
dress and carriage styles, permissible technology, resistance to change, and social distance from the larger
world. Moreover, each of their twenty-six hundred
church districts (or congregations) holds final sway
over religious and social practices. This decentralized
ecclesial authority has spawned some twenty-six hundred different ways of being Amish in America. Yet
amid this diversity, many common traits—beliefs and
rituals—still make it possible to talk about "the Amish"
as one social group.

A few other terms also warrant clarification. The
Pennsylvania Dutch–speaking Amish refer to outsiders
as *English*, which I do as well in these essays. Further-
more, I use the word *communal* to describe Amish
religious and social life, not their economic practices.
The Amish hold private property and compete in public markets. *Plain* is a descriptor for the distinctive

dress and lifestyle of certain Anabaptist groups, including the Amish and the most traditional Mennonites and Brethren; the term appears in the commonly used phrase *Plain people*.

Lastly, quotations from Amish people in the essays come from my field notes and Amish source documents. Most speakers remain anonymous. For those named, I use first-name pseudonyms out of respect for a long-standing tradition of humility whereby the Amish avoid having their names appear in public media. Any first name repeated refers to the same person. I do use the real full name of Amish authors and Amish people who previously appeared in public media or records.

✤

In a time when civil discourse is raw and coarse, when social discord and deceptions disturb us, when the scourge of political corruption and mass shootings anger us, when technology threatens to overwhelm us, when violence is our default for solving conflict, when loneliness is the norm, when addictions and suicide rates soar, and in days when our social fabric seems torn asunder—our Amish friends have much to teach us.

WHAT THE AMISH TEACH US

*

RIDDLES

Negotiating with Modernity

Attendees at my public lectures and classes sometimes ask, "How did you get interested in Amish studies?" The short answer is the riddles of Amish life. The long answer begins with my personal story.

I was born in 1945 a few weeks after atomic bombs exploded over Hiroshima and Nagasaki. My Mennonite parents were farmers in Lancaster County, Pennsylvania. We were plain-dressing, progress-minded Mennonites. Our church buildings were simple meetinghouses without steeples, yet we drove cars, farmed with tractors, and supported higher education. Mennonites and Amish shared a European Anabaptist heritage. But by the 1950s many Mennonites, including my family, considered the Amish antiquated, left-over relics of the nineteenth century. We scoffed at their old-fashioned practices and assumed that they were headed for extinction.

In 1971, I began teaching sociology at Elizabethtown College (in western Lancaster County), and by 1984, I was casting about for a new field of research. Early that summer, Paramount Pictures began filming *Witness*, an Amish feature film, in Lancaster County. To the dismay of Amish leaders, the Hollywood company recruited Amish people to advise them and provide props for the shooting. Some Amish churches ordered members to stop participating. Those who refused were excommunicated. The controversy surrounding the film received heavy media coverage. All of this piqued my interest in Amish studies.

The contradictions of Amish life in the mid-1980s intrigued me. Their practices seemed illogical and outright hypocritical to some people. Why, for instance, did the Amish seek the care of physicians but forbid their children from becoming one? Why did they ban telephones from their homes but permit them in private outdoor booths? Why did they forbid car ownership yet allow members to hire rides in motor vehicles? These riddles mocked common sense and bewildered Amish fans and skeptics alike. Likewise, the rapid growth of Amish communities, both in Pennsylvania and across the country, confounded me.

Hoping to solve these puzzles, I began to explore this

question: How are the tradition-laden Amish—who spurn electricity, automobiles, and higher education—able not merely to survive but to thrive amid a modern, high-tech society?

Delving deeper into Amish culture, I searched for a system of logic in this hodgepodge—a web of meaning that might make sense of the conundrums. After completing some interviews and field observations, I stumbled onto an idea that has helped me interpret the riddles of Amish life. The Amish were, I thought, negotiating with modernity: they *rejected* some aspects of modern life and *accepted* others.

For example, they rejected radios, television, high school, church buildings, and salaried ministers but accepted small electronic calculators and artificial insemination of cows. And more recently, many churches, but not all, accepted gas grills, state-of-the-art birding equipment, LED lights on buggies, and battery-powered hand tools.

Plus, Amish people *bargained* with other aspects of modernity—striking compromises on mechanical devices and social practices. The bargaining happens in two ways.

First, as one member explained, "We *Amishize* things so they fit into our Amish way of life." Educational leaders Amishize elementary schools by eliminating technology and constructing a curriculum that reflects Amish values. On the technical side, some "engineers" neuter computers (stripping out video games, Wi-Fi, and online access) to make them safe for Amish use.

The second type of bargaining permits *access to* but not *ownership of* certain things. For instance, the church prohibits tapping electricity from the public grid. However, an Amish woman may use public grid electricity to light her dried flower shop if it's in a rental building. Similarly, a member mowing grass for an English motel can use the motel's riding mower but cannot own one at home.

And the bargaining continues. One Amish woman barters with her English neighbor for access to her computer to buy products on Amazon in exchange for some produce and pastries. In another realm of Amish life, most churches have an Amishized mutual aid program to cover health care costs in lieu of having commercial health insurance.

I find the negotiating fascinating. It's a way of mediating social change, of arresting assimilation into American society. Besides, the give-and-take with the outside world shatters the stereotype of an insular, separatist clan.

And, yes, there are reasons—historical, moral, practical ones—that guide the decisions to reject, accept, or bargain. In particular, the taboo on owning motor vehicles aims to promote local horse-drawn travel to preserve a close-knit, face-to-face Amish community.

This dickering with modernity enables the Amish to protect their traditional identity while still reaping some of the fruits of progress. It keeps the world at bay, while at the same time partaking of some of the world's achievements. The Amish aren't intimidated by modernity. They engage it, scrutinize it, and screen it—refashioning it to serve their community.

This was the first and most important lesson the Amish taught me.

※

TWO

VILLAGES

Webs of Well-Being

As I wrapped up a discussion of *Everything Is Wonderful*—an Amish-themed drama about forgiveness that was fraught with conflict—an elderly gentleman stood up to speak. "Professor, it's about the village." About the village? I wondered. "Yes, I'm a retired psychiatrist, and my research found that the most satisfied people in the world live in villages. These Amish act like villagers."

The old gentleman was on to something. Contented people may live in villages, although the link between contentment and village life is a complicated one. Even so, we do know that people in small-scale communities, villages of one sort or another, have dense social networks. We also know that robust social ties enhance psychological well-being.

The Amish version of a village is usually called a church district. I prefer the term *church-community* to accent the communal reality of Amish life. A church-community consists of twenty to forty families who live near each other. These small communities are the cornerstone of Amish society—somewhat equivalent to a parish, synagogue, temple, or congregation in other faith traditions. There is no commonly held property. An Amish church-community has roughly 140 to 175 people, and about half of them are under eighteen years of age. When membership grows too large, the families divide into two communities.

Amish church-communities have geographical boundaries, such as roads and streams. The extent of a church-community's square mileage varies with its population density and occupations. Predominantly farming communities may stretch several miles from side to side. If people leave farming, less land is needed, and the footprint shrinks. In compact church-communities, many families live within a half mile of each other.

Amish families never live in isolation. If they plant a new community far from home, several families move together. There are some twenty-six hundred Amish church-communities in North America. Some of them stand alone. Others are part of a loose affiliation of other church-communities.

The social fabric of an Amish church-community is similar to villages worldwide with one exception: Amish people live interspersed with English neighbors, sometimes on adjacent properties. English people participate in joint civic affairs and engage in commerce with their Amish neighbors. The English, however, don't join in Amish social and religious life.

The families in a church-community worship together in their homes every other week, rotating from house to house throughout the year. Without church buildings or other common facilities, much of Amish life centers on the home. Residents of a church-community cannot join another one unless they move into its territory.

The church-community is the ceremonial and social hub of the Amish world. Church services, baptisms, weddings, funerals, fellowship meals, education, and a host of social activities bring folks together. The church-community wraps family, school, work, church, club, and precinct into one ethnic enclave. The social fabric of the church-community, with its crisscrossing threads, is a thicket of dense and deep human ties.

Amish life requires real face time—the original social medium—body by body, eyeball to eyeball. "Visiting is our national sport," said one Amish man with a chuckle. Drop-in visits and stop-by chats happen anytime, anywhere. A lot of walking, bicycling, and getting around on push scooters makes it easy to visit. Visiting energizes people and bonds the community together. And with all the real face time, members don't need faux chat time: instant messaging, tweets, or Facebook. Besides, said one member, "the Amish grapevine is faster than the internet."

Unlike the sharp split between personal and public life in modern society, Amish people "can't hide much, not in church, not on the farm, not in our community," admitted a grandfather. "The whole neighborhood knows everything because everything is so transparent." In the mind of one elder, their church should exemplify a closely knit Christian community, living, working, and worshiping together. Here the members know each other and care for each other every day of the week.

Even so, Amish life isn't idyllic. Squabbles happen. People get upset with each other. It takes a lot of forgiving and forbearance—putting up with petty stuff, giving in and giving up—to make a church-community thrive.

Still, despite the bickering, there's mutual caring aplenty in the hearts of members. When disaster strikes, people come. If your house burns down, they show up. If you lose a child or spouse in an accident, they show up. They also come if a flood ruins your store. If your business is on the verge of collapse, three trustees will show up with power of attorney to avoid bankruptcy at any cost. People do whatever they can, and they will keep on doing it as long as help is needed, even for life.

And if adversity strikes someone else in the church-community, you will show up—you know you will because it's part of the implicit church-community pact. Even if you don't particularly like the person or family hit by the hardship, you will show up. Everyone does. It's just the Amish way.

Leaders urge members to "avoid accepting aid, handouts, grants, or subsidy payments from the government . . . because the Bible teaches us to work for a living. We believe it's unscriptural and demeaning to become dependent upon the government to support us financially."

Amish social security may be messy, but it's reliable, and that's a big deal for people who opted out of government-run social welfare. The Amish said no to federal Social Security back in 1955 and, more recently, to Medicare. They don't pay in or take out. They're on their own. They pay all other taxes—income, property, school, and so on.

Even today, the Amish have no people who are homeless, no one sleeping on sidewalks or in barns. No one is on the government dole. Governments can make policies. They can fork out money and build housing, but they can't provide personal care, the kind that's patient, persistent, and adaptable to all the complexities of a person's life.

In the end, no matter how much misfortune you've caused others or have suffered yourself, the church-community will—like a continuing care community—take care of you. It will look after you until the end, and it will bury you with dignity when you die and kiss the earth goodbye.

❧

Those of us who yearn for a taste of Amish life might try to strike out on our own. We might move to a rural area, start canning vegetables, observe silent prayers before meals, have a midwife deliver our babies, dress in simple clothing, rid our home of video, give up indoor air conditioning, cut the cord to the public grid, pull our children out of school after eighth grade, and even travel by horse and buggy. But—and it's a big *but*—maintaining those practices alone in an isolated rural area would be difficult, if not impossible, without the support of a village of like-minded families.

We might think that we can make it on our own, that we're smart enough to figure out everything by ourselves, and that we have the stamina to go it alone. Going it alone has its freedoms, but they get old after a while; and too often loneliness waits at the end of the road.

The singular truth of the Amish argument is this: life is a communal project, one that requires the proverbial village. We all need a village of one sort or another. People with robust networks are healthier and enjoy life more than those with sparse social ties. In short, a sturdy fabric of interdependence fosters psychological well-being. So it's not surprising that, even with all its quirks, the Amish favor village life.

-❋-

The national "weaver" movement is a village-type venture, spawned by Weave: The Social Fabric Project at the Aspen Institute. It's devoted to repairing America's social fabric, which is being ripped apart, in their words, by social fragmentation, distrust, division, trauma, and exclusion.

New York Times columnist David Brooks, a champion of this movement and the founder of Weave, prods us to consider the role we play. Are we ripping apart the social fabric or weaving it tighter? Every time we stereotype a person, we weaken the civic fabric; every time we invest in village life, we strengthen the social cloth. Do we want to be a ripper or a weaver?

The lesson from Amish country is clear. Villages matter. Having a community matters, having a circle of support, however small, matters. Healthy villages require stitchers, not freeloaders, and weavers, not rippers.

We can't replicate an Amish village. But we can invest in our own kind of village—a civic group, a faith community, a neighborhood coffee klatch, a friendship cluster—and make it stronger. If we already have a village, we can help it thrive, and can mend it when it frays. If we don't have a village, we can join one or cobble a new one together with some friends.

THREE

COMMUNITY

Taming the Big "I"

Sam and Sally were unusually quiet as the clip-clop of their horse, Hank, took them toward the Millers' home. It was seven thirty on a Tuesday morning. There was little to say. They knew that within eight hours, their lives and those of their children could change forever.

Their church-community was gathering for its fall Holy Communion, to be followed by the ordination of a new minister. Sam sensed his pulse rising already. He knew that the same thing was happening to a dozen other men under forty-five years of age who were also likely nominees. One of them would be selected in what to outsiders looks like a random lottery. But to insiders, the biblical casting of lots is the holiest and highest ritual of Amish life—as God Almighty reaches down from heaven to select a new shepherd of the flock.

No one applies for this job. And no one wants it. Moreover, no one can turn it down or back out. Before baptism, every young man agrees to serve if called by God. No pay or training comes with this lifelong duty. Only a grievous sin, illness, dementia, or death offers an exit.

There is no applause or celebration for the new minister, who joins the leadership team of two ministers, a deacon, and a bishop. The announcement of the new minister's name releases a flood of sobs and tears in the emotion-charged moment. Everyone knows that for years to come, they are stuck with him and he with them. Anyone unhappy with the outcome can argue with God. Sam was one of the six nominees that day, but as the Amish say, "The lot didn't hit him."

The casting of lots to select leaders has served Amish churches well over the ages.

‡

Ordination is the ultimate act of yielding to the church-community. It's part of the pact—the unwritten agreement—among members of a church-community. Young adults on bended knees implicitly endorse the lifelong covenant at baptism when they promise to renounce self-will, the world, and the devil. Baptismal candidates who renounce those things and embrace the church receive lifelong benefits of security, belonging, and meaning.

The pact is countercultural. It flips the moral authority of the individual upside down. In popular culture, the *self* comes first, followed by family or various kinds of groups—religious, political, leisure, civic, and so on. In Amish life, the highest moral authority is the church-community, followed by family, and then the self. The schoolroom motto JOY teaches children that *J*esus is first, *Y*ou are last, and *O*thers are in between.

The moral primacy of self or group marks the divide between Amish and American values. Consider, for example, these questions: If you are thinking of buying an e-bike or a smartphone, would you consult your imam, pastor, rabbi, or priest before making the purchase? Likewise, if you are invited to serve on the zoning board of your local municipality, would you consult a religious leader before deciding?

The Amish pact has religious guidelines. Each Amish church-community has an unwritten map of regulations known as the *Ordnung*. Twice a year, the church-community affirms the guidelines in a business meeting. The meetings are conducted with the understanding—based on the teaching of Jesus in Matthew 18:18–20—that his Spirit guides those making decisions. Most importantly, the collective choices made on earth are ratified in heaven.

No one needs a reminder of the taken-for-granted customs of Amish life—that men grow beards and shave their upper lip, that horse-drawn travel is the Amish way, that high school is not necessary, and that women don't wear makeup. These issues were resolved long ago. Current issues such as power lawnmowers, smartphones, and the use of computers and electricity for businesses are more likely to be discussed at the twice-a-year affirmations.

Heaven's blessing on the Ordnung gives it hefty authority. This makes it hard to change long-established traditions. Moreover, the divine endorsement covers all regulations related to daily life, including dress, technology, and transportation. As professor Karen Johnson-Weiner says, in effect, "the Amish are always in church."

✻

The title of an Amish essay, "Taming the Big 'I'" tells it all. Although self-denial may sound repressive to us, it's at the heart of the pact. For Amish people, self-denial means "sacrificing our own selfish interests and desires in our service to God." One leader writes, "We are part of a group, and as such we must be willing sometimes to make personal sacrifices in order to serve the overall benefit of the group." It's not surprising that humility tops the list of Amish virtues.

In Amish lingo, pride is a label for unfettered individualism. One Amish publication puts it starkly: "Pride . . . seeks to exalt the self." Amish people cite numerous scriptures to show that God hates a proud look, considers a proud heart an abomination, resists the proud, and gives grace to the humble. "It was pride," said one minister, "that brought down the world the first time at the flood," a reference to the biblical story, when God grieved the prideful acts of humanity and wiped all but Noah and his family from the earth.

Pride, in Amish eyes, elevates the individual above the community. Proud people call attention to themselves; they are pushy, bold, and forward. Besides, proud people tack their name on everything, draw attention to themselves, and take credit for everything. A humble member declines public recognition.

How one walks, shakes hands, removes one's hat, and drives one's horse signals humility or pride. A swagger or a quick retort betrays a cocky spirit. An aggressive handshake and a curt greeting disclose an assertive self. A gentle chuckle, a hesitation, and a slow and thoughtful answer embody the spirit of humility.

Pride has many faces. One of the Ten Commandments forbids making a graven image or a likeness of anything (Exodus 20:4). Historically, the Amish applied the injunction against likenesses to photographs, which legitimated their well-known taboo on personal photographs. They especially consider a face-on, posed photo to be a sign of pride.

✣

Yielding to the community, however, doesn't smother individual expression and choice. The church doesn't choose your spouse or your job or tell you where to live. Nor does it place any restrictions on food. Creative self-expression flourishes—from quilting patterns and embroidered handkerchiefs to colorful stickers on children's lunch pails, from gardening to hobbies, from farming to crafts.

My Amish friend Amos says, "The idea that we give up all freedom of choice and that the community decides everything is a myth. Even if you decide to let the church decide, that in itself is a choice." He recalled that buying a home "involved many choices for us. How big, how many acres, what price range? Do we buy acreage and build, or do we buy an existing house? Do we buy at public auction or private? And so on."

Then, getting a bit more personal, he smiled and said, "The church doesn't tell us to wear boxer shorts or briefs or to go to McDonald's or Burger King. I could go on and on about a myriad of choices we make on a daily basis, like Pepsi or Coke, vanilla or butter pecan. You get the idea." In his mind, there's room aplenty in the pact for individual choice and creativity.

-❋-

The pact summarizes the Amish argument: setting limits is the foundation of wisdom. Without boundaries, individuals become arrogant and self-destructive. And although restraints may appear to stifle individual freedom, they in fact grant dignity to the individual. For Amish people, yielding to the collective wisdom of the community brings security, belonging, and meaning.

The community provides a home, a secure place where you always count, with a people who will always care. Community means belonging to a people, having an identity, and knowing who you are and that you're not alone. And participating in a religious community fills life with meaning because it's tied to a larger mission.

FOUR

❋

SMALLNESS

Bigness Ruins Everything

On a field trip early in my Amish research, I interviewed a man who ran a small carpentry shop with his son. Near the end of the stand-up interview, amid the sawdust and shavings, I asked, "Do you ever think of expanding your shop?"

"Nope, never."

"Why not?

"Bigness ruins everything." And he rattled off some examples of big things gone awry.

It was just three words: *bigness ruins everything*. A cute throwaway quip? Not this one. It had intellectual depth and breadth. I never forgot it, and I soon came to realize that it's writ large across Amish life.

From egos to social units, everything is little—small congregations, small schools, small farms, small dairy

herds, small businesses, small everything—except sizable families. An Amish businessman explained: "My
people look at a large business as a sign of greed. We're
not supposed to engage in large businesses, and I'm
right at the borderline now and maybe too large for
Amish standards."

Amish society revolves around a local, small-scale
community that is bound together by a web of crisscrossing relationships. The same circle of people has
overlapping ties in family, neighborhood, church, and
work. People relate to one another in multiplex roles.
For instance, Ben may be your uncle, neighbor, co-
worker, friend, and fellow church member.

When you meet your neighbor Jessica, you already
know dozens of things about her. You know, for instance, that Jessica's father died when he fell off the
roof of a barn when she was seven, that her aunt bakes
the best apple pies in the community, that the church
excommunicated her grandfather for betting on horse
races, and that she has only one kidney. And Jessica
knows that your older brother never joined the Amish
because he wanted to fly airplanes, that your aunt hob-
bles because a horse kicked her as a child, and that
you dated an English boy before you joined the church
and married Amish.

Everyone in the church-community learns these
scraps of information as they grow up. People rarely

mention them now, yet the stories still color their thinking when they interact. In such a thick-context culture, many things can remain unsaid because everyone already knows each individual's biography.

In the words of one Amish woman, "Everybody knows everything about everyone else." Everyone knows if you miss a church service. People enter the meeting place by gender and age. Your absence will be conspicuous because those who walk in front of, or behind you, will notice. And the word—that you were sick, at a cousin's out-of-state wedding, or visiting one of your married children living in a new Amish community—will quickly spread at the fellowship meal after the service.

Although such transparency repulses modern spirits raised on the rights of individual privacy, thick-context cultures attest to the big-fish-in-a-small-pond proverb. Small-scale units, interestingly, make individuals "big" psychologically. Each person has an intimate spot in a small circle of friends. No one gets lost in the crowd. No one is anonymous. Each person has an identity, a secure place, and a sense of personal dignity.

Hidden beneath the public bonnets and buggies that spell out Amish separation from the world is an even more striking rejection of modernity: *the absence of bureaucracy*. It's missing everywhere in Amish life. The Amish world has no central headquarters. No public relations office. No national conventions, no synods, and no president or chief executive. "We don't have a pope," said one man, "just a lot of bishops!" The absence of a Vatican frustrates journalists who reach out to me wanting contact information for the "Amish PR office" or the "head bishop of the church."

Amish bishops in some affiliations meet periodically for informal discussions. Yet even if they agree on an issue, its interpretation rests in the hands of each local bishop. Under the "home rule" guideline, the church-community has the final say on church regulations.

Why does bigness threaten Amish society? One man described his fear this way: "Our life thrives with a small group. Once you get into that big superstructure, it seems to gather momentum, and you can't stop it." Pointing to a growing organization that the bishops had curbed, he said, "It became self-serving, like a pyramid. Suppose we get a rotten egg leading it sometime? He can do more damage and wreck in one year than what we built up in twenty. That's why the bishops curbed it."

Whenever one person gets too much power or too much financial advantage, bigness spoils the egalitarian spirit of the church-community. The preservation of Amish society requires small person-to-person communities. Bureaucracy is the antithesis of organic thick-context communities. Supersized organizations permeate modern life with their central control, rigid hierarchy, and formal rules, roles, and job descriptions.

Even though the Amish carpenter who claimed that bigness spoils everything had never read academic studies on the negative effects of bureaucracy for employees—alienation, lack of control, and feeling like a mere cog in a machine—he intuitively understood how bigness could imperil his community.

Although the Amish have steered clear of bigness within their ranks, they still faced a predicament: how to cope with the state, the epitome of bureaucracy. Lacking a collective voice hampered Amish leaders in their efforts to deal with the state's regulatory tentacles. The absence of an Amish counterpart to the pope also frustrated government officials. Federal and state agencies had little patience for hearing complaints from dozens of different church districts.

To address the problem, Amish people created the National Amish Steering Committee. Without any traces of bureaucracy, this loose network of leaders embodies Amish values yet still has enough clout to engage with government officials effectively.

Representatives from states with sizable Amish communities meet twice a year. The volunteers receive no compensation for their work, and when they decide to retire, they find their replacement. Moreover, they are laymen—not ordained leaders. Hence, the committee does not speak for the church as a legal body.

Over the years, the steering committee has effectively lobbied for Amish interests in conflicts over schooling, slow-moving vehicles, Social Security, zoning, environmental protection, and workplace safety, among other issues. It provides a unified voice to negotiate with state and federal officials.

Amish efforts to protect their twenty-six hundred church-communities from the ruinous effects of bigness attest to their deep and often hidden separation from modern society. Their respect and advocacy for smallness prompts the rest of us to ponder what might be lost in our habit of hankering for the biggest.

FIVE

❋

TOLERANCE

A Light on a Hill

For the Jewish scholar Yuval Noah Harari, monotheism gave birth to bigotry. In his view, the idea of one God "was arguably one of the worst ideas in human history." Monotheism, he suggests, bred intolerance, which in turn inflamed religious persecutions and holy crusades.

We may think that a Christian group such as the Amish, especially one grounded in long-standing change-resistant customs, would be steeped in intolerance and draw sharp lines of distinction between their religion and that of others. At least that's what I expected to find when I began researching Amish life. I was wrong.

Fifty-year-old Rebecca, a single Amish woman, taught me a big lesson shortly before I published *The Riddle of Amish Culture*, my first book on the Amish.

Coincidentally, Rebecca was staying overnight in our home once a month as I was completing the manuscript. We happened to live near her chiropractor's office some thirty miles away from her home. She traveled by public bus, which involved several transfers and a two-day round trip.

We soon became friends. She invited my family and me to a meal at her home, which she shared with her two single sisters, and kindly took our two young daughters on a buggy ride. Rebecca was eager to see my manuscript. So when I finished it, I gave her a copy and asked for her feedback. When she returned the next month, I eagerly inquired, "So what did you think?"

"I only found one problem," she said, "but it's a big one."

It must be awful, I feared, since it was the only problem she had found in a hundred thousand words detailing a host of Amish customs.

"You said that the Amish think everyone else is going to hell, but that's not true," she said. She was clearly annoyed that I had written such a thing.

"I don't recall ever writing those words," I replied.

"Well, they're right here in chapter two," she said, pulling out a marked-up page. She pointed to my words in the text: "Taking their cues from the Bible, the Amish divide the social world into two categories:

the straight, narrow way to life and the broad, easy road to destruction. Amish people embody the straight and narrow way of self-denial while the larger social world is on the broad, easy road to destruction."

"Yes," I said, "but that doesn't exactly say that Amish people think everyone else is going to hell."

"But that's what it *means*, and we don't believe that."

"Well, I didn't just make it up; it comes from the Bible. Jesus advises his audience to go in the narrow gate because the masses go in the broad gate that leads to destruction," I said, referencing the text of Matthew 7:13.

She dug deeper. "But that verse doesn't say *who* is entering which gate. You wrote that 'the larger social world is on the broad, easy road to destruction.' That means that we think everyone else is headed to destruction, going straight to hell."

I was startled by the strength of her conviction. "Well, what do you believe?" I asked.

"We don't believe in judging other people. That's God's job. Jesus told us not to judge other people because we will be judged like we judge them," she said, referencing Matthew 7:1–2. "We don't think we're the only ones going to heaven. It's up to God to decide who goes where."

Convinced, I asked her for suggestions on how to fix it. I fiddled with some new wording and then decided to replace "destruction" with "vanity and vice" and came up with this line: "The larger social world represents the broad, easy path of vanity and vice."

"That's perfect," she said, "and it's true because it doesn't say that we think English people are going to hell." Then she pivoted. "Can you please call the printer and tell them to change that quickly before they print any books?"

I assured her that I would. And I did.

Only one wrong word—*destruction*. Only one among a hundred thousand words! Surely she must have seen some dubious cultural details, but for Rebecca, those didn't matter. What mattered was an outsider's offensive insinuation that her people were bigots who condemned others and even usurped God's role in balancing the scales of justice.

I marveled at the surprising subtext of our conversation. A fearless eighth-grade-educated woman speaks out and stands up against a well "educated" professor to defend her people and the truth. A brave woman sets aside all the values of patriarchal deference and submission that she learned as a child. And she musters up the courage to tell the truth to a man, a supposed scholar, who had jumped to a conclusion without verifying it with his informants, a man who was fortunate enough to have her call him on it.

Rebecca also confirmed that her people do not

proselytize or evangelize. "Doing those things is also judging," she said, "because we'd be saying that our religion is better than theirs and our way is better than theirs. We think that we should be like a light on a hill. That's how we should witness," she said. This oft-mentioned metaphor in Amish circles comes from Jesus's words in the Sermon on the Mount, where he urged his disciples to be a shining light to the world that glorifies God (Matthew 5:14–16).

Shortly after the tragedy on October 2, 2006, in the West Nickel Mines School, where an English neighbor shot ten Amish girls, killing five of them and then himself, I interviewed the parent of a child who had died there. In the aftermath of the shooting, the Amish forgave the man and his family. Speaking of how this forgiveness story made headlines in hundreds of media outlets worldwide, the father said, "Our forgiveness reminds me of being the light on the hill. Sometimes some of our people think we should do more evangelistic work or begin a prison ministry, but our forgiveness story made more of a witness for us all over the world than anything else we can ever do." Another parent agreed: "Maybe this was God's way to let us do some missionary work. Maybe God used the media to help spread the Word."

Amish churches do not engage in evangelism or operate mission agencies, although some members give contributions to non-Amish mission projects. And members of Amish groups serve others outside their community by participating in various Anabaptist service and disaster relief organizations.

Amish people hope that their collective way of life will glorify God. In sermons, writings, and conversations, they emphasize the importance of letting their light shine. Amish writer Benuel Blank put it this way: "A Christian can be a good witness in many ways. Living a good example has led more people to Christ than any amount of talking has ever done."

The do-not-judge-others mantra, from the lips of Jesus, reflects the bedrock of Amish faith. Tolerance destroys bigotry. Humility generates respect for other ways of believing.

SIX

SPIRITUALITY

A Back Road to Heaven

A few weeks after the 2006 shooting at the school-house in Nickel Mines, Kendra, the daughter of a friend of mine, called. "Do you think the Amish are saved?" she asked. The members of her Christian evangelical congregation were having a lively discussion about the salvation of Amish people. The debate had been sparked by how quickly Amish people had forgiven the man who shot ten of their daughters, killing five of them.

Kendra noted that some people thought that their forgiveness alone showed that Amish people were saved. It was unthinkable that anyone without genuine Christian faith would have been able to forgive so quickly. Amish forgiveness surely exemplified the highest virtues of Christian love, mercy, and grace. If people who practice those virtues aren't saved, then who is?

Still, other members of the congregation disagreed. Some who had Amish neighbors said that Amish people rarely spoke about personal salvation. These members accused the Amish of believing that their obedience to church regulations would save them instead of relying solely on God's grace. For evangelicals, eternal life depends on confessing their sins and accepting Jesus as their personal Savior and God's unmerited grace.

Salvation—the redemption from sin and reunion with the divine on earth or in eternity—is a core belief of many religions. With heaven and hell at stake, some evangelicals seek to evangelize Amish people to save them from eternal perdition. So it's not surprising that the Amish salvation controversy stirred strong feelings in Kendra's congregation.

A gap divides evangelical and Amish views of salvation. The two spiritualties rest on different assumptions and use different dialects to describe salvation. One spirituality is individual-centric. The other one is community-centric.

In the twentieth century, individualism and personal choice became hallmarks of American culture. Influenced by mainstream society, evangelical theology adopted individual-centric language to describe salvation. Conversion narratives focused on individual choice, decision-making, certainty, and control. Personal stories were public, expressive, and emotive.

Evangelical watchwords are akin to these: "I was born again on [date], when I accepted Christ as my personal Savior." The personalized wording fits an individual-centric worldview. Likewise, the phrases—personal salvation, personal Savior, personal Bible study, personal testimony, personal witness—all articulate one's *personal* feelings, agency, and choice in ways that accent the *individual* rather than the *community* as the center of redemptive activity.

With some exceptions, the Old Order Amish were untouched by evangelicalism in the twentieth century. Their religious spirituality remained community-centric, embedded in long-standing traditions reaching back to their Anabaptist forebears in the sixteenth century. Amish writer Benuel Blank writes, "The first Anabaptists believed in a living hope. They believed in a hope that is alive." Even so, they weren't sure of reaching heaven. "They left that up to the perfect judgment and mercy of God."

Amish spirituality is couched in the language of humility. The Amish understanding of salvation rests on a "living hope." This phrase permeates Amish thought with a calm confidence that God will be a just and merciful judge. Grounded in profound trust, this stance acknowledges that God, not humankind, is the arbiter of such weighty eternal matters.

Although evangelicals celebrate personal experience, evangelism can also induce anxiety. How, for example, can one be sure of eternal salvation beyond any doubt? Spiritual uncertainties have spawned shelves of books on the assurance of salvation, as well as catchphrases such as "I'm sure I'm saved" and "I know I have eternal security."

Bold claims about an assurance of salvation border on arrogance to Amish ears, for salvation is God's business. Amish people remind us that even the scripture declares that not everyone who says, "Lord, Lord," will be saved; only those who *do* the will of God (Matthew 7:21). Besides, opining about one's eternal salvation is considered prideful. "Humility," says an Amish bishop, "never exalts itself. Never boasts about salvation."

Amish people hesitate to talk of an assurance of salvation because they tie it to a lifetime of faithful living. If conversion is a onetime event, unrelated to how one lives in the future, it's tempting to declare that "once saved, always saved." The Amish link salvation to ethics and faithful practice. They cite Jesus's teaching that good trees bear good fruit (Matthew 7:17–24). Amish people do confess that Jesus is the Son of God who died for their sins, but they also believe that, as his disciples, their lives must exemplify his ethical practices. "Feeling and experience is bubble and froth," explained an elder.

In some ways, evangelical and Amish vocabularies are analogous to the different symbolic languages used to express love—gifts, presence, touch, fidelity, and acts of kindness. Evangelicals speak a language of individualism that stresses beliefs, certainty, feelings, and experience, whereas the Amish speak a language of communality that stresses patience, humility, community, and ethics on their back road to heaven.

The heart of Amish faith throbs with the quiet rhythms of genuine spirituality. An admonition in one of their devotional books articulates their sentiments of faith: "In your conduct be friendly toward everyone and a burden to none. Toward God, live a holy life; toward yourself, be moderate; toward your fellow men, be fair; in life, be modest; in your manner, courteous; in admonition, friendly; in forgiveness, willing; in your promises, true; in your speech, wise; and out of a pure heart gladly share of the bounties you receive."

Members of Kendra's congregation will not likely choose to walk on the Amish back road to heaven. Still, they may have a new appreciation for the different dialects spoken on the various roads to heaven.

✳

SEVEN

FAMILY

A Deep and Durable Bond

At about six on a crisp Monday morning, the smell of coffee, toast, and scrambled eggs greeted me as I entered Rachel's small kitchen. Her husband, Leon, was already sipping coffee at the table. The elderly couple had kindly offered me lodging during an October field trip to New York's Amish country. Glancing about the kitchen, I saw five open greeting cards standing alongside some ready-to-mail envelopes on a countertop. Not sure of their purpose and hoping to start a conversation, I said, "You have a lot of cards there."

"Yes, each one's for the birthday of one of our grandchildren," said Rachel. "They need to be mailed on different days this week."

"Five in one week?"

"It's not that many every week. Some weeks there aren't any, and one week there's seven."

"So how many grandchildren do you and Leon have?"

"Eighty-three." She said, with a big smile of delight. Eighty-three!

Rachel explained that most of their children live near them, but some live in Pennsylvania, where they had lived previously. They had eight children, and some of their children had more than that.

"That's a lot of grandchildren," I said. "It must take a lot of work to get all those cards, write the messages, address them, and mail each one on the right day."

"I get the ones for each week ready to go by Monday morning, so that makes it easier to keep them straight," said Rachel. She asked me how many grandchildren my wife and I had.

"We don't have any," I replied.

"None? Oh, I'm so sorry for you, so sorry."

"Well, I'm only fifty-five, so we still might have some. We have a married daughter."

"Well, I surely hope so," she said. "We really enjoy ours."

Amish writings and sermons laud the premier value of family. It's what life's all about: starting a family and raising children who, in turn, will produce more. "Our children are the only crop we can take along to heaven," quipped one father.

For a few moments, Rachel had poured out the deepest joys of her life to an outsider—one whom she had never met before and would likely never see again. Without restraint, she spoke about her crop of grandchildren and genuinely empathized with my barren harvest in a modern society whose values she didn't share.

Amish families are large. From their perch on their family tree, Leon and Rachel's immediate family, including their eight children and their in-laws and all those grandchildren, totals 101. A typical extended family—assuming an average of seven children per family—for a fifty-five-year-old grandmother may exceed four hundred people. This tally includes her parents, her siblings, her children, her aunts and uncles, her first cousins, her nieces and nephews, and the spouses of all these people, plus her husband's side of the family.

Although some of the kin may live out of state, most reside within twenty miles of one another. Some may live next door or just down the road. A young mother told me, "I don't have to worry about babysitters. I have three relatives nearby, and at least one of them is usually free if I need to drop off a child on my way to town."

The high priority given to family and reproduction originates from the biblical imperative to be fruitful and multiply (Genesis 1:28). This exhortation makes it unthinkable not to marry or to marry but intentionally remain childless. Some couples who are barren may adopt a child or provide short-term care for English foster children. A community that forbids divorce has few single-parent families. It's not unusual, however, for widows and widowers to remarry, which often produces blended families. Some families are dysfunctional. I know of rare cases where husband and wife live in separate quarters on the same property. And sometimes discord divides extended families.

Family life prepares children for collective living. Growing up in a large family is a minor league for adult communal life. The child learns a key lesson early on: "I'm not the center of attention. I'm not the hub of the family wheel. I'm just a spoke. I'm a vital spoke, but many other spokes help hold this wheel together to make it spin. And that's what matters: all the spokes working together to spin the wheel as smoothly as possible."

Living in a big family requires a lot of giving in and sharing of toys, beds, clothing, and attention. It involves waiting to see if any of your favorite dessert will be left when the dish reaches your end of the table, waiting to speak, and knowing that your birthday is just one of perhaps a dozen in your immediate family.

The extended family network offers informal support and wisdom across the life span from birth to death. When a child is born, one or two women show up and manage the household for several days. Family folklore seasoned by time provides recipes for cooking and remedies for conditions ranging from common ailments to depression. It's hard to overstate the importance of the family system. It's the ballast that gives individuals a sense of place, stability, and durability.

·✳·

Every person stands in three overlapping social webs: church-community, family, and friends, woven together by threads of duty and care. When tragedy, death, or other trouble strikes a nuclear family or an individual, these webs spring into action. Amish people—who have collectively opted out of government assistance—rely on these social webs to assist with medical needs, disabilities, fires, storms, and other troubles. These personalized versions of social security provide a reliable safety net.

One poignant example is the Beiler family, who lost a twenty-year-old son in a tragic snowmobile accident in Colorado, nearly two thousand miles from their home in eastern Lancaster County.

Aaron Beiler called me one evening with a request: "I'm trying to write a book about my son's accident. Could you come and help me?" We met at his home, and he explained how "our people responded with overwhelming love and care." On the first Sunday after the funeral, thirty-two families visited to offer support and share their grief, and an average of twenty-five visitors a day came by over the next two weeks. In addition, the Beilers received over six hundred sympathy cards and letters as well as flowers from Amish friends near and far. Such an outpouring of care is not unusual after a death—especially an unexpected one of a young person.

This kind of response is the abundant love that young people know they will miss if they leave the Amish faith. They know that family and friends will not only show up when tragedy hits but will hang in for the long haul, even assisting over the years, if needed. This outpouring of care touches deep primal instincts. This is the love that makes it hard for young people, or adults for that matter, to turn their back and walk away forever from a community that—despite its many shortcomings and squabbles—will care for them regardless. This everlasting nitty-gritty love evokes a deep tribal belonging, a longing that keeps most of the wayward-leaning souls at home.

·❋·

EIGHT

CHILDREN

At Worship, Work, and Play

Child-rearing habits play an essential role in preparing children for adulthood. With large families and extended family connections, children are almost always part of the scene. Amish life is family life, and children abound. And though they aren't pampered, as sometimes happens in English culture, they are loved and cared for. Moreover, from a child's perspective, they are part of a flock of siblings, cousins, and friends in their church-community, which provides ready partners for work and play. The following vignettes from my field notes offer glimpses of children in church, at breakfast, at work, and at play.

·❋·

Amish friends had invited me to attend a church service that met in the daylight basement of their home.

A five-foot-wide aisle divided the meeting space into separate sides for men and women. They faced each other as they sat on backless wooden benches. As a guest of honor, I walked in with the older men and sat on the men's first row, facing the women's first row.

Eight-year-old Lydia and I faced each other across the five-foot aisle. She sat on the women's first row near her grandmother. Probably a third-grader, Lydia was somber, settled, and content. Apart from turning around and kneeling on our benches for a lengthy silent prayer and singing some ten-minute-long hymns, we looked at each other for nearly three hours. I winked once. She didn't respond, not with the tiniest trace of a smile. She never flinched, never glanced away, just looked and looked at me.

Lydia had been through these rituals some two hundred times before. A friend of patience, she remained calm and fearless—unintimidated by a strange older man facing her for three hours. How had Lydia, in eight short years, learned to master a level of emotional control that few adults ever attain?

I lost sight of Lydia after the service. She likely joined her friends for lunch and socializing. After lunch, a group of twelve- to fifteen-year-old boys grabbed a football and ran off to a grassy field to play flag football—yelling, teasing, laughing; they demonstrated how Amish youth can suddenly shift from quiet reverence to boisterous play.

❊

It was five thirty on a cold February morning in Iowa. An Amish family had invited me to stay with them for two days during a research trip. Now I was leaving to visit New Bloomfield, another settlement in Iowa. I washed, packed my bags, and walked out to the kitchen. Susie, my hostess, was watering some small plants in a mini greenhouse on the sunny side of the family room. She asked me to take greetings to some of her friends at New Bloomfield.

Her three young daughters were preparing breakfast. An eight-year-old flipped pancakes on a hot grill. She was also in charge of her younger assistants. A six-year-old pulled yogurt from the fridge, set several cereal boxes on the table, and looked for some syrup. Meanwhile, a four-year-old placed silverware at each plate. The eight-year-old corrected her when she forgot to put a spoon at one place setting.

While Susie and her daughters attended to home and food, father Abner and a son returned to the house after finishing chores in their goat barn. They washed, and we gathered at the table. Then we had a long silent prayer. The shuffle of Abner's shoes signaled the "amen."

As we ate, Susie, Abner, and I talked about New Bloomfield. They offered suggestions about whom I should visit and how to find their homes. The children listened intently, learning a lot about New Bloomfield. As we finished our food, Abner said, "We'll have devotions, and then you can go." He reached for a Bible and read about ten verses of scripture in German. Then he said, "Now we'll kneel at our chairs while I read a morning prayer from one of our old German prayer books." Every morning, the day begins with prayer and reflection, immersing the children in a religious worldview that filters through their activities for the rest of the day.

And then I was off to New Bloomfield.

✤

In early June, I stopped at a small Amish produce farm near my home to buy some strawberries. I arrived about ten minutes before the nine o'clock opening. The retail operation was inside the tack room of an old barn. A country road ran between the house and barn. From the parking lot at the front of the barn, I saw the parents and their children in the strawberry patch down a slope, five hundred yards away on the house side of the road.

Soon, nine-year-old Andy came running up the slope along the road to the barn, looking for an express wagon. He found it and took it back to the strawberry patch, where the parents stacked layers of trays—full of retail-size boxes of strawberries—on the wagon. The trays wobbled. So he asked his seven-year-old sister to hold them while he pulled the wagon. Their four-year-old sister, without any instruction, pushed the wagon from behind. Together they came quickly up the slope along the shoulder of the road and then crossed over to the barn.

Andy opened the door to the retail shop. Then he and his seven-year-old sister carried the trays to the display shelves. Shortly after nine, he waved me into the store. He answered my questions about this particular variety of berry and operated the cash register for my purchase. He did this all without guidance or direction from his parents.

-*-

One evening in late November, an Amish historical committee invited me to meet with them to discuss one of their projects. We met at the home of a committee member. He had remodeled the old farmhouse to accommodate three living units: one for his family, one for his married sister's family, and a small apartment for their elderly parents. During our two-hour meeting, eight boys ages six to ten, who had accompanied their fathers to the meeting, roamed the three living areas and their basements. The homes provided a cavernous space to play hide-and-seek. The boys

were noisy, especially when they found a hidden com-
rade. Even so, they weren't destructive. Nor did they
disrupt our meeting. They played at will without adult
supervision, except for an occasional "Not so loud" from
one of the fathers when the children came through the
large family room where we were meeting.

Without access to television, computers, and video
games, Amish children engage in a lot of improvised
play—outside in summer and inside during the winter.
That November evening, the boys knew and stayed
within the permissible boundaries of noise and speed.
Yet they enjoyed remarkable freedom as they shared
two hours of free-range play.

✻

NINE

PARENTING

Raising Sturdy Children

In recent years some baby boomers were surprised to learn that their grandchildren had enrolled in Adulting 101 workshops. From the University of California, Berkeley, to Temple University in Philadelphia, thousands of college seniors were enrolled in noncredit classes to learn how to survive in the adult world. Life skills—how to do laundry, cook a meal, change a tire, manage a budget, rent an apartment, and prepare taxes—had somehow slipped through their educational preparation. Adulting curricula address the unmet needs of students who feel unprepared to cope in a world of adults.

When my Amish friend Amos heard about this, he said, "I feel a tinge of pity. But I'm grateful they have the opportunity to learn things we just take for granted." I told him that every society raises their children in different ways. Adulting workshops help modern youth succeed in an individualistic culture. Amish child-rearing prepares children to thrive in a communal society. Amos smiled. "It's funny and ironic that the Amish and English each pity each other on a lot of things," he said. "You guys probably pity our children for the way we raise them. We start early and learn by doing."

Pity aside, Amish children grow up fast. They become adults quickly. Amish leaders and writers consistently emphasize that a parent's first and highest duty is to raise children who love and obey God and the church. A widely cited poem in Amish circles, "The Upbringing of the Child," informs parents of their sacred task. The poet starkly reminds them that if they fail in this endeavor, they "face the danger of being a total stranger to heaven":

> When early discipline is lacking,
> Times will come, which bode no good.
> Sinful nature must be tamed,
> Else conflict taints the neighborhood.
> What you teach them early on,
> They'll later bring to mind.
> Habit has tremendous strength;
> Both the good and the evil kind.

Cooperation is the cornerstone of communal life. So it's not surprising that a child-rearing publication would declare that "a child's self-will *must be given up*." If parents don't tame the sinful nature of a child, they fear that the child will grow up to be headstrong and cantankerous—behavioral traits that clash with communal life.

I asked one mother how she knows when to start disciplining a disobedient child. She explained, "If children are old enough to fold their hands at prayer time, they are old enough to be reprimanded with light spanks." Another mother told me, "When children are about two years old, their will needs to be broken. If it's not done at that stage," she said, "they will likely become disobedient and rebellious adults. The spanking helps to correct them and make them nice." One woman emphasized, "We love our children. When we spank them, it's a discipline to help them control their minds. When spanking, we don't get angry at them."

To Amish thinking, a small amount of discipline by age four eliminates countless hours of argumentation later in life. An Amish woman who worked as my research assistant for six months asked me one day, "Why do English children argue so much with their parents? Our people don't do that. Our children never talk back to their parents. We think that's very rude."

When asked what is the most important thing to teach a child, a grandmother said, "To obey and to work." The adage "Idleness is the devil's workshop" circulates on Amish lips and implies that God blesses an unfailing work ethic.

Work training starts young. In her "Tips on Training a Two-Year-Old," an Amish mother writes, "Children love being involved! We are to love them, train them, guide and nurture them. God has given these souls into our care." The writer advises mothers to greet two-year-olds in the morning with a "warm hug and a kiss from the heart." She then describes in detail how to involve them in six household chores—packing lunches, setting the table, washing dishes, changing a diaper, sewing, and cleaning. She concludes, "Thank your helper sincerely, even if there is a mess to clean up. Let your child feel your love." A mother of six boys whom she'd trained to do dishes told me, with a twinkle in her eye, "They'll be in high demand when they start dating, and they'll be good husbands."

Leaders underscore the importance of families working together. One parent explained how he had stopped working on a construction crew and bought a deli stand in a farmers' market "so the family could work together; it's a family thing." Regardless of the task, everyone pitches in and does their part with family-based jobs. And family work is often invigorated by pranks, jokes, and teasing.

Responsibility looms large in child-rearing. When a family works in a garden, a child may have a specific row of green beans to weed and later pick. In the barn, a child may care for a particular calf, sweep the back section of a shop, or feed and water a coop of chickens. Some children are responsible for caring for a particular pet or doing a specific chore, such as washing the carriage every Saturday. To earn some spending money, siblings may raise guinea pigs or grow cantaloupes to sell.

In some homes a twelve-year-old girl might have the responsibility of baking pies for a social gathering. A boy or a girl might harness a pony to a small cart to haul some produce to a friend's house two miles away. Others may guide a horse pulling a hay rake or a small harrow in a field. These tasks require quick decisions if the animal bolts.

Children are accountable for doing their tasks well. Work teaches them skills, as well as common sense and lessons from their mistakes. Children gain personal satisfaction from a job well done and develop the confidence to tackle more demanding tasks. Work sends an implicit message to a five- or six-year-old: Your job is important. Our family needs you. You make our family stronger. Working together creates a sense of security and identity and underscores even a young child's contribution to family well-being.

This favorite schoolroom verse captures the goal of Amish child-rearing:

> I must be a Christian child,
> Gentle, patient, meek, and mild;
> Must be honest, simple, true
> In my words and actions too.
> I must cheerfully obey,
> Giving up my will and way.

Patient. Meek. Obedient. These qualities are essential to prepare children for adulthood in communal life. Of course, developing the habits of diligence, responsibility, and resilience lays a solid foundation for success in both the Amish and English worlds.

We may understandably wince about spanking as a form of discipline and about repressing emotions, yet about nine out of ten of these children will embrace the Amish world as young adults. None of the nine will become lawyers, scientists, or entertainers. Still, lest we worry about lives wasted, some Amish-raised youth will program 3D printers, engineer new inventions, and operate profitable businesses, as they and others find hundreds of other ways to lead satisfying lives in Amish society.

·•·

TEN

EDUCATION

The Way It Should Be

In May 1991, Lucian Niemeyer, a recently retired business executive from Philadelphia, and I visited a one-room Amish school in Lancaster County. This was his first visit to an Amish school. We sat together at two empty back-row desks. After observing the classroom for two hours, Lucian's eyes filled with tears. Shaking his head, he looked at me as he wiped his tears with a handkerchief. "Don," he said, "I can't believe it. This is the way it should be. It's amazing to see it right here amid our modern commotion."

At Clear Valley School, the nineteen-year-old teacher, Sadie, and her seventeen-year-old assistant, Erma, skillfully taught thirty-two pupils in eight grades. Colorful chalk drawings filled one side of the blackboard. Individual posters, each with a pupil's name, were fastened to a wall. Pink streamers fluttered from the ceiling, and seventeen straw hats hung on pegs on the back wall. The open windows offered a view of cows and horses in a nearby pasture. After Sadie read Psalm 100, the pupils repeated the Lord's Prayer and sang a German hymn, followed by an English one. Then the classes began.

Sadie taught clusters of students from two grades at a time, sometimes at their seats and other times at the blackboard. The first- and second-graders practiced math with flashcards while the seventh- and eighth-graders calculated percentages and the diameter of a circle. Other students quietly helped one another. Five or six hands would shoot up whenever Sadie posed a question. When students completed their worksheets correctly, Erma pasted smiley faces on them.

Clear Valley School might have looked like a century-old Amish school to an outsider. But it wasn't. Until the 1950s, Amish students across the country went to small, rural *public* schools. They had English peers and teachers. In some areas, Amish fathers served on local school boards. For the most part, parents were satisfied with the small public schools.

All of that changed abruptly in the mid-twentieth century. One-room schools were vanishing. The rise of large consolidated schools required busing students who lived in rural areas. That, plus the push for high school education, a more extended school year, more years of compulsory education, and strict enforcement of attendance, frightened Amish people.

The engineering logic of specialization and efficiency —so successful in producing radios and Model T Fords on the assembly line—was being applied to education, resulting in large educational factories for hundreds of students. Amish leaders worried that the consolidated high schools, designed to homogenize diverse students into a common national culture, would destroy their communities. They wanted schools designed to prepare Amish youth for successful careers in Amish life, not in mainstream society.

What kind of schooling did the Amish want?

They were happy with what they had—the small, locally controlled public schools within walking distance of home. They wanted teachers who were trustworthy and sympathetic to Amish values and rural ways. They wanted a basic curriculum that terminated with eighth grade—one absent of worldly philosophies, evolution, science, and sex education.

Parents fretted that their offspring would get haughty and lazy in public high schools. The paramount fear lurking beneath all the concerns was that modern education would lead Amish youth away from faith and farm and undermine their way of life.

Some school battles had flared up in Pennsylvania,

Ohio, Indiana, Iowa, and Kansas in the late 1930s.
These intensified with the end of World War II as
public educators argued for stronger doses of a demo-
cratic "vaccine" to prevent America from ever falling
into the hands of a tyrant as had happened in Ger-
many. The Amish were resolute in their resistance.
Hundreds of parents in various states were arrested
and served short stints in prison. In one Pennsylvania
township alone, officials arrested more than 125 parents, some of them as many as five times.

Why did the docile, mild-mannered Amish resort to
courts, petitions, and politics to preserve their values?
Why were these gentle people willing to sit behind
bars? Why were they so unyielding?

Amish people reacted in those ways because, in
their eyes, they faced an epic battle with modernity for
the souls of their children. It was a David and Goliath
showdown. Never before had Amish people across the
country so stubbornly resisted modernization. Their
convictions were nonnegotiable. Gradually, various
types of state-by-state changes accommodated Amish
concerns. Amish parents quietly began operating one-
and two-room schools. Still, the issue of compulsory
high school festered until a case from Wisconsin landed
in the United States Supreme Court.

Finally, in 1972, the court, in *Wisconsin v. Yoder*,
ruled in their favor, stating that "there can be no as-

sumption that today's majority is 'right' and the Amish and others like them are 'wrong.' A way of life that is odd or even erratic but interferes with no rights or interests of others is not to be condemned because it is different."

Three hundred Amish schools were well established by the time of the court's decision. Over the years, these schools have played an important role in reproducing Amish values and strengthening communal solidarity and identity. They have helped Amish society thrive. These islands of provincialism may not stretch Amish consciousness, but they provide secure and safe settings for the emotional and social development of children.

Clear Valley School gave witness to the steely convictions of Amish parents half a century earlier, parents who fearlessly fought for their right not to be modern. Today, some two thousand one- and two-room Amish schools stand as the antithesis of advanced, specialized education.

So what did Lucian mean when he said, "This is the way it should be"? He saw students engaged in learning. He saw a quiet orderliness and heard a low-level hum as pupils in some grades worked together. He saw curiosity and some subtle humor. He saw respect for a nineteen-year-old teacher who never once raised her voice. He saw security and contentment on the faces of pupils who had a sense of belonging, the kind of belonging and well-being that scholars in recent years have found correlates with academic achievement.

That's what he meant, and why he cried, that day in May.

꙳

ELEVEN

APPRENTICESHIP

An Old New Idea

One particular riddle of the Amish that vexed me for many years was their entrepreneurialism: How do Amish entrepreneurs learn to start and manage a successful business? How do they acquire the ingenuity to create enterprises that garner annual revenues of $1 million or even more? Some oversee manufacturing plants, others operate retail stores, and still others manage sizable construction companies. Thousands of these operations are running every day across America.

Amish business leaders, both men and women, are products of one- or two-room Amish schools. Some of them even had the same teacher for all eight grades. The schools typically have no technology except for a battery-operated clock and sometimes a photocopier.

These young entrepreneurs never attend high school or college and never take a course in accounting, administration, or human resource management. None of them holds an MBA. Not a single one. Amish entrepreneurs are scrappy, innovative, and hardworking. So how do they acquire the requisite skills to run profitable businesses that serve their people and compete successfully in public markets?

The pieces of that puzzle suddenly came together for me on a sweltering August day. I was standing behind a barn near a forty-five-foot silo and watching two Amish farmers operate a machine designed to chop and blow green stalks of corn up a tube alongside the silo. The gooseneck at the top of the tube dropped the chop into the silo, where it would ferment into sweet-smelling silage for winter feeding.

A tractor on steel wheels provided power for the operation. The tractor's hydraulic system controlled an experimental device on the chopper. This Amish-made device pulled large bundles of cornstalks off the wagon and fed them into the chopper-blower to expedite the process and reduce manual labor.

After functioning for a few minutes, the hydraulic system failed, and everything shut down. Because the farmers had no expertise in hydraulics, they called an Amish hydraulic shop about ten miles away. The mechanic who arrived that morning was a fourteen-year-old lad named Aaron. His dad, who owned the shop, was busy with other projects, so he sent Aaron. Aaron quickly crawled under the equipment to search for the problem, and within an hour he had it fixed.

How did this young man become so skilled in hydraulics that he could troubleshoot and fix a complicated new system? The answer is simple, so simple that I'm embarrassed it took me so long to solve the puzzle.

Ever since he was a toddler, Aaron had spent a lot of time in his dad's shop. By the time he was four years old, he was pushing a small broom to clean the floor at closing time. When oil spilled onto the floor, Aaron would get a rag to wipe it clean. By the time he was eight, he was able to assemble clamps on hydraulic hoses and do other similar jobs. All the while, he was paying attention, listening, observing, ever eager to grow up and do adult work.

He learned to take responsibility. When he made a mistake, his father asked him what it had taught him and showed him how to avoid making it again. If he slacked off, he faced a reprimand. Meanwhile, Aaron moved through the grades of his one-room school. In fact, he had finished his formal schooling and begun to work full-time in his dad's business a few months before being sent to the silo that day.

Aaron's story is not unique.

Take ten-year-old Mary, who sits at the receptionist's desk of her family's furniture shop every Saturday morning. She answers the phone and responds to any questions about store hours or directions. She also files records related to various products and sales. Besides learning a bunch about furniture and customer service, Mary, a native speaker of Pennsylvania Dutch, has gradually acquired some competency in English as she converses with English customers who frequent the store.

Nine-year-old Sylvia welcomed me with a big smile when I entered her mother's greenhouse in search of a Mother's Day flower. She seemed to know the names and locations of all the plants. Without consulting her older sister or her mother, Sylvia took me to a large area filled with geraniums, and grinning with satisfaction, she explained the different varieties.

It was Saturday afternoon, and eleven-year-old Eli was managing the cashbox at the checkout of his family's weekly chicken barbecue. The distinctive sauce and low prices, plus the opportunity to witness an Amish family in action, attracted hundreds of customers, who also bought pastries and jams. At the checkout, Eli added and subtracted without a calculator. He knew his multiplication tables from memory. With paper and pencil, he totaled the cost of each customer's bill and mentally calculated their exact change—something English high school graduates might be challenged to do without the calculator on their phone.

Not all Amish apprentices are under the supervision of their parents. Some trainees are employed by a next-door neighbor, an aunt, a cousin, or a friend of the family. The arrangements are informal. There's no office of Amish apprenticeship. No one assigns an apprentice to a mentor. Everyone—children, youth, adults—knows the tradition. It just happens. But it works.

In the Amish world these old-fashioned apprenticeships matter. They are the seedbed for budding entrepreneurs. The Amish have always endorsed a hands-on, practical education that emphasizes trial and error, hard work, responsibility, and accountability. This commonsense system has run smoothly for decades, so it's not surprising that the Amish continue to rely on it for training their youth.

What is surprising, however, are headlines such as "Why Colleges Need to Embrace the Apprenticeship" in the *Chronicle of Higher Education*. This multipage article tells the story of Noel Ginsberg, CEO of a plastics company, who, after funding college scholarships for years, realized that they were not a ticket to success. In an about-face, he now argues for apprenticeships with a built-in relevance that inspires students to succeed. In recent years, many articles in higher education literature echo this trend, suggesting that some sectors of American higher education are finally catching up to the Amish.

TWELVE

❈

TECHNOLOGY

Taming the Beast

Can humans control technology? Should we try, and is it even possible? Our addiction to devices and our inability to shake their grip grow daily. Technology guru Kevin Kelly, in his book *What Technology Wants*, fears that the enormity and the cleverness of our creation has overwhelmed our ability to bridle it.

"Technologically impaired"—that's what "Weird Al" Yankovic calls the Amish in his satirical song and music video "Amish Paradise." Like other people, he perpetuates a pervasive myth: the Amish shun technology. They do not. They're not impaired. And they're not Luddites. They *selectively* use, adapt, and create technology to serve the needs of their community.

When we turn to the Amish, we discover their grit in grappling with the beast and wrestling it to the mat.

They're not willing to accept whatever modernity brings their way. Their eye is on long-term planning—on the downstream consequences that technology might have on their community and its future.

Their struggle with motor vehicles offers a compelling story about taming technology. When Americans developed an insatiable appetite for Henry Ford's cars, the Amish didn't bite. They had long driven horse-drawn buggies and, since the late nineteenth century, ridden on trolleys and sometimes boarded trains for long-distance trips.

As the cars rolled off Detroit's assembly lines, the Amish kept driving their horse-drawn carriages. Localism—supported by a horse culture that tethers members close to home—has always ruled supreme in their society. Horse conveyance supports a face-to-face, small-scale, oral community and keeps Amish people out of cities.

Any invention that promised self-propelled mobility spelled trouble for them. The automobile freed people to travel independently—whenever and wherever they pleased. Auto travel symbolized the spirit of American individualism and independence by liberating people from train and trolley schedules, breaking the bounds of geography, and threatening the provincialism of rural life. Amish youth could drive away to urban centers of vice. Adults could go to worldly sites of employment, where they would mingle with strangers. In short, the car clashed with the core of Amish life.

The new contraption threatened to fragment Amish communities, woven tight by the constraints of horse-drawn transportation. The car's centrifugal pull would surely tear the bonds of community asunder. Easy access to cars would shatter and scatter a communal way of life. This daunting symbol of modernity promoted individualism, freedom, acceleration, mobility, and autonomy—all of which promised to imperil a separatist way of life.

As autos arrived in rural areas, Amish leaders soon forbade owning one or holding a driver's license. Now, a century later, car ownership still remains banned. Anyone who buys a car faces excommunication. Moreover, "when people leave the Amish," said one member, "the first thing they do is buy a car."

Is owning a car sinful? That's the question I asked Bishop Levi while we sat in his living room. "Cars aren't immoral," he said after a pause. "We don't think people who own them are going straight to hell. It's what cars will do to our community. It's about the next generation."

Strike through the image of the stuck-in-the-mud Amish. Such stereotypes gloss over their keen grasp of the disruptions caused by cars and their strategic vision for communal survival—a grasp ably summarized by

Bishop Levi, a farmer educated for eight grades in a one-room school. The taboo against the automobile aims to protect the community from the car's long-term impact on its connective social tissue. Although the Amish may appear technologically impaired, Bishop Levi surely wasn't strategically impaired.

Despite the taboo, the car brought temptations. By the 1920s, the Amish had slowly begun to strike a bargain with modernity. In particular circumstances (health, business, emergency), members were allowed to request a ride in a neighbor's car or truck. With this Uber-like early form of ride sharing, the Amish gradually drew a line between *access* and *ownership*.

Several factors spiked their *use* of motor vehicles in the mid-twentieth century: the collapse of the rural trolley system, the geographical expansion of Amish settlements, and the growth of Amish-owned businesses. Carpentry crews needed transportation to construction sites. Small-scale manufacturing shops required access to trucks for receiving raw materials and shipping their products.

To meet these and other needs, English neighbors on a partial or full-time basis provided transportation— a customized rural taxi service—for the Amish. The drivers charged by the mile, plus waiting time if stranded for a day or two at a faraway funeral or wedding. These "taxis" ranged from cars to trucks to passenger vans. This bargain has kept motor vehicles at bay by controlling their adverse side effects, while still granting the Amish access to the convenience, economic benefit, and means to reach family members in distant settlements.

The agreement reminds everyone that vehicles should not be entrusted to individuals. Doing so would quicken the pace of life, erase geographical limits, weaken social control, and eventually ruin their community. Horse-drawn transportation encourages people to work and socialize near home, which fortifies the bedrock of Amish society, church-communities.

Traveling by van fosters community by building social capital. As with many things, the Amish do it together. Traveling in groups reduces costs. Vanloads of Amish people are, in essence, portable subcommunities, keeping their worldview alive on daily rides to work and during visits to relatives in far-flung settlements. They are traveling at highway speeds while socializing with like-minded others as they go.

Controlled access to motor vehicles keeps faith with tradition while giving just enough freedom to maneuver in the larger society. It allows use of modern technology without being enslaved by it or allowing it to fray the social fabric. The Amish took the car, the charm of modernity, on their terms and struck a deal that enabled them to employ it to enhance their community.

The primary fear, for any new technology, is how it might harm their community over time and what it will lead to next. An Amish obsession with steel wheels illustrates this concern. Tractors and farm wagons must have steel wheels, which prevent them from traveling on public roads. The Amish fear that a homemade wagon-bus on tires, pulled by a tractor with tires, might lead over time to owning a pickup truck and eventually a car.

The takeaway here is not about cars. It's about having the courage to appraise the long-term social impact of technology and to tame it, if necessary, so that it serves people in a controlled and humane way.

-❈-

THIRTEEN

HACKING

Creative Bypasses

On a late October afternoon in 2015, I was standing in an Amish lantern shop surrounded by a dozen students from my Amish culture seminar. The shop's business card says it manufactures and sells "Mantle Lamps, Lanterns, and Glass Shades."

Ever since Amish churches forbade members from using 110-volt current from public power lines in the 1920s, lantern shops have flourished. An Amish man explained, "It's not so much the electric that we're against, it's all the things that would come with it—all the modern conveniences, television, computers. If we get electric lights, then where will we stop?"

Elam, the owner of the lantern shop, pulled samples off the display shelf as he explained the evolution from kerosene oil lanterns to the latest propane gas ones found in many Amish homes. He also described how safety and efficiency had improved over the years. Even so, the widely used propane lanterns (similar to a Coleman camping lantern), fueled by portable canisters, are a hot, noisy fire hazard.

Elam then invited us to see his son Gid's project on the second floor. We followed thirty-year-old Gid up the steps and stood around him, staring at his project. "So here we have ten 3D printers," he said. "We run them twenty-four six, never on Sundays."

I had never seen a 3D printer before. There I stood, a college professor in an old-fashioned lantern shop staring at ten machines that Gid had programmed for his project. This eighth-grade-educated man, who had taken an apprenticeship with a self-trained Amish computer wizard, was introducing a professor and his students to state-of-the-art technology that we had never seen before. Meanwhile, through a window, we could see horses hitched to carriages, impatiently stamping their feet in the parking lot below. The ironies of this were spinning in my head as Gid explained that the 3D printers—powered by 48-volt electricity from batteries charged by a solar panel—were making a plastic adapter. An adapter?

For decades, the church had permitted batteries to power flashlights, portable lanterns, and headlights on buggies, among other things. When battery-powered cordless tools became popular in America in the late 1980s, Amish people bought them by the dozens for using in homes, shops, and construction work. Gid knew that thousands of Amish people had battery-powered DeWalt tools such as drills, sanders, saws, and hedge trimmers. However, each type of machine required a battery designed for it. He imagined a vast Amish market if he could devise a way to run many small devices from one rechargeable, portable battery. The adapter, manufactured by his 3D printers, did precisely that.

One part of the adapter connects to a DeWalt battery. A standard electrical cord from an appliance plugs into the other side of the adapter. The adapter makes it possible to power a host of small devices—printers, typewriters, copiers, alarm systems, ventilation fans, LED lights in homes and shops, plus diffusers for essential oils—from a rechargeable battery. A home or school without access to public grid electricity can use the adapter to power a fan or a copy machine. Likewise, a family can illuminate rooms in their home with LED lights and scuttle their dangerous old gas lanterns. The portable adapter can power different plug-in devices in a house, shop, or barn.

Gid was hacking by creating a workaround without violating any long-standing church regulations. He respected the rules (no public grid electricity and the longtime acceptance of batteries). His new gadget could network commercially available products (3D printer, battery, small devices) without violating any norms of the church's moral framework.

❦

A handful of Amish hackers in Illinois who called themselves the Wildcats worked every Friday night to solve a problem faced by families that use propane gas for running stoves, refrigerators, and portable lights.

The pounds-per-square-inch pressure, or psi, of propane gas is identical for stoves and refrigerators. However, propane lamps require a much higher psi. If the hackers could engineer the burner valve on a lamp so that it burned brightly and quietly with the same psi of stoves and refrigerators, then all the gas appliances in a home could draw from the same propane tank. Achieving this would eliminate the old portable propane lamps.

After an engineer from a nearby university declared that goal impossible, the Wildcats tripled their efforts. Finally, after six years of experimentation, they accomplished their mission. The new device not only eliminates the dangerous old lamps; it can also connect all the wall-mounted gaslights in a home-distribution system.

❦

A cottage industry of Amish "engineers" across the country who enjoy tinkering with technology has developed hundreds of roundabouts to public grid electricity. These bypasses provide several alternative sources of energy—low-voltage battery, solar, compressed air, or a combination—to achieve results similar to standard electricity. Some people jokingly call the alternatives "Amish electric."

Amish church-communities set their own regulations on technology. The most traditional ones reject both compressed air and propane lanterns. Thus some workarounds welcomed in progress-minded communities are forbidden in others.

To convert a standard electrical appliance, like a kitchen stand mixer, to air requires replacing the electric motor with a small air motor. An air compressor, powered by a diesel or small gasoline engine, forces pressurized air through a hose to spin the mixer's motor. One man, speaking about a new electric blender, said, "I can't use it until I Amishize it by ripping out the electric motor and installing an air motor."

❊

A couple setting up housekeeping in a progress-minded community can find these "Amish electric" options in Amish publications, whose ad pages promise all sorts of converted convenience.

"Need a clothes washer? We have options. An automatic washing machine powered by a battery and solar. Or an air-powered automatic washer. Or a rebuilt Maytag wringer washer powered by air. If your community rejects airpower, we can help. We have a rebuilt Maytag, powered by a flexible driveshaft that you can run with a portable power unit outside your house.

"What about a clothes dryer? Our air-powered high-speed stainless steel spinners are the next best thing to electric dryers. One of our customers claimed, 'The spinner makes the clothes so dry you can jump right in them on a hot day!' Another one called the spinner 'the best thing since sliced bread!'

"How about some kitchen appliances? We have food processors, blenders, cake mixers, and other air-powered stuff. When it comes to refrigerators and freezers, we've got propane gas and solar-powered options.

"Something for your home office? We can set you up with electric typewriters powered by batteries. And word processors, you know, Amishized computers, stripped of video, Internet, games, and sound. And by the way, we have Plain cell phones—flip phones with no Internet, no texting, no games, no camera, none of that bad stuff.

"Or, are you worried about a traffic ticket in super slow zones? No problem. We have a speedometer for your buggy. It tracks current speed, average speed, maximum speed, trip distance, trip time, and total distance, plus a clock. All for fifty-five dollars."

---*---

Horse and progress. That pair of words sounds like an oxymoron. In Amish country, they flow together nicely on Horse Progress Days. This annual event rotates from state to state each summer. It showcases the latest work of hackers who build horse-drawn farm equipment. The festival attracts some ten thousand spectators, including English draft horse fans.

At Horse Progress Days, which is staged on a large farm, attendees see the new machines performing demonstrations in the field. Some products include Amishized commercial hay balers and harvesters adapted to be pulled by horses. The vast majority of equipment built by Amish businesses—pre-engineered to meet church regulations—is both Amish-friendly and field-ready. The array of new equipment includes mowers, cultivators, plows, sprayers, spreaders, harvesters, wagons, and rakes.

---*---

Hackers take charge of technology. They mold it into the Amish moral order. Good hackers balance respect for tradition while seeking alternative ways to pursue progress. Hacking breeds a can-do attitude—one that says, "We can find a way to get around the obstacles and make this project work." Hackers have an enter-prising, innovative mindset. And besides, they have a lot of fun tampering with technology to make Amish life more productive and satisfying. Hackers exemplify how a culture of restraint, ironically, spurs innovation and invention.

❊

FOURTEEN

ENTREPRENEURS

Starting Stuff

"Entrepreneurs start stuff," says Wayne Wengerd, founder of a farm machinery company in Dalton, Ohio. Amish entrepreneurs have started a lot of stuff! They've started twenty thousand businesses, from one-person operations to sizable ones like Wengerd's Pioneer Equipment company with several dozen employees. Hundreds of microenterprises, from manufacturing and services to trades and retail, populate the Amish landscape.

Most of these businesses were started after 1970. As land prices rose and the Amish population grew rapidly, many families sought non-farm income. Now, more than two-thirds of households depend on it.

Starting a business in Amish society is another form of hacking, since entrepreneurs face obstacles galore.

Cultural taboos forbid litigation, public grid electricity, motor vehicles, Sunday sales, formal education beyond the eighth grade, commercial insurance, and air travel. Add to those the core Amish values of humility, smallness, deference to others, and separation from the world. Moreover, local church proscriptions vary regarding access to telephones, computers, and use of social media and the internet for business operations and promotion. Communal living requires humility. Entrepreneurs who highlight their achievements and take credit for success may be chastised for pride.

All of these factors stifle starting stuff; they hamper start-ups that are trying to compete in an aggressive, high-tech marketplace. Thus, success requires a lot of hacking. And all the hacking must align with the regulations of the business owner's church-community.

❦

Amish entrepreneurs include a vendor of popcorn.

"Prepping for a party? We have just the thing for you: Emma's Gourmet Popcorn. We have fifty flavors, the likes of Amish Peanut Butter Schmeir, Birthday Cake, Buffalo Blue Cheese, Caramel Macchiato, Cheesy Crab, Chocolate Almond Bliss, Chocolate Caramel Espresso, Chocolate Peanut Butter, Cinnamon Bun, Cucumber Dill—and more.

"We pop each batch of corn by hand. It's a gourmet specialty and not a mass-produced product. We use non-GMO popcorn. Many of the flavors are gluten-free. Baking takes much longer because we are dedicated to bringing you the best possible gourmet popcorn with a perfect crunch and melt sensation in your mouth!"

Nancy, the proprietor, explains that her mother, Emma, started making popcorn in a small shed in 2006. When Emma retired in 2010, Nancy took over. She added more flavors and moved the operation into a two-car garage on the ground floor of her bi-level home. Now doubled in size, the operation includes a small retail corner, stacked with popcorn samples, where customers can watch employees hand-drizzle flavors over batches of popped corn.

Customers can choose from four sizes of bags (holding from three to thirty-two cups), party platters, snack trays, and large refillable tins. The shop ships popcorn to customers and wholesales it to retail outlets. Emma's promotes its products on Facebook and a website operated by a third-party vendor. It's a home-based shed-to-success story.

In the mid-1970s, Wayne Wengerd also began tinkering in a shed—not with popcorn but with plows—in Dalton. He hoped to design a new high-quality, horse-drawn plow since all the factory-made ones since the mid-1950s had been built for tractors. By 1977 he had made twenty-five new horse-drawn plows. They sold like proverbial hotcakes. A year later, he started a machine shop in a small building.

Today his booming company manufactures some forty different types of horse-drawn machinery with multiple models: wagons for farming, pleasure, and parades; buckboard buggies (the Amish version of a pickup truck); horse and pony carts; and large round hay balers, tillers, harrows, mowers, plows, and manure spreaders, to name but a few. Some of the small equipment targets the needs of produce farmers and orchardists.

Pioneer Equipment ships its machines to customers across North America. Dealers in various regions of the country promote Pioneer products. The company customizes equipment to fit the regulations of different Amish affiliations by placing steel wheels or rubber tires on wagons, for example. In addition to Amish people, many English customers—orchardists, produce farmers, draft horse farmers, and horse enthusiasts who want covered wagons or stylish carriages for parades, festivities, or horse club outings—buy Pioneer products.

At first glance, Pioneer's factory looks and sounds typical, but there is one exception: Amish electric. Compressed air, hydraulic, and batteries power the manufacturing operation. Large diesel engines run the air and hydraulic pumps. With nearly fifty employees, many of whom are family, Pioneer Equipment is one of the largest Amish companies.

-∗-

Success stories in Amish entrepreneurship are not unusual. Several studies report that less than 5 percent of Amish businesses fail in the first five years of operation. Compare that with 50 percent of American small businesses that collapse within sixty months of start-up. Even with creative hacking, how is it possible to achieve a 95 percent survival rate in the face of church-based constraints?

If Amish cultural norms hinder microenterprises in many ways, they also invigorate them. Resources in the communal reservoir counterbalance the cultural constraints. These cultural resources include a rigorous work ethic, entrepreneurial skills forged on the farm, and a frugality that minimizes overhead costs. A pool of ethnic and family labor brings shared values to the workplace. And a small-business culture with few employees increases their commitment and job satisfaction because they're directly involved in planning, decision-making, and production.

Moreover, self-employed Amish business owners and their Amish employees are exempt from paying into Social Security. This lowers payroll costs, as does the fact that few businesses have pension plans because the church cares for the aging as needed. Additionally, if a business falters, three church-appointed trustees will nurse it back to health and, if necessary, use power of attorney to avoid bankruptcy, which the Amish deplore.

Plus, every Amish entrepreneur has a valuable asset—a free, powerful brand. Oddly, the No Sunday Sales signs posted by retail businesses; the cultural constraints on telephones, public grid electricity, and motor vehicles; the peculiar practices of using postal mail instead of email, of answering phones only at certain hours, and of using compressed air and hydraulic force to power machinery—all proclaim the uniqueness of Amish wares and bestow on them the widely recognized AMISH brand.

Emma's Gourmet Popcorn doesn't use Amish-raised corn, but knowing that Amish hands have touched the chocolate-covered morsels in a cottage industry makes them taste even more scrumptious. The Amish label stirs up nostalgic feelings for the past—images of early Americana, small neighborhoods, and strong families—and it invokes sentiments of durable products handcrafted with care by hardworking people who have spurned the modern world.

The Amish brand is so potent that some English poachers use a buggy logo or phrases like "Amish Country" to sell non-Amish products. Like the trademark Starbucks, the word *Amish* and the horse-and-buggy emblem perform magic in the marketplace.

Amish businesses have many unique features that help them prosper. Surprisingly, some of their old-fashioned recipes for productivity and success are applicable to non-Amish businesses. In his book *Success Made Simple*, Erik J. Wesner distills some of these well-seasoned lessons that small-business owners everywhere can take from Amish entrepreneurs about how to create a thriving enterprise.

✤

FIFTEEN

PATIENCE

Slow Down and Listen

An old Amish saying—the early bird gets the worm, but the second mouse gets the cheese—reminds the cheese-loving Amish that patience guides their journey. Patience marks the mood of every Sunday service, with its slow hymns that seem to go on and on forever. And patience permeates the silent prayers before and after every meal.

Every buggy that plods along a modern highway proclaims PATIENCE. "The horse is our pacer," explained an Amish man. "We can't speed up like you can in a car. Our horses set the pace for life and slow things down." Riders in an open-window, gadget-free buggy can see and smell the countryside and nod to friends along the way.

The most traditional Amish do not set their clocks

ahead an hour each spring or back each fall, as other Americans do. These slowpoke Amish—who favor slow time, God's time, regulated as it is by the rising and the setting of the sun and the changing of the seasons— appear antiquated. Yet a national twenty-first-century movement, now gaining momentum, aims to end Daylight Saving Time in order to "make everyone's lives just a little better . . . a little happier . . . a little safer," reminding us that the stuck-in-time Amish are once again ahead of the rest of us and are already living lives that may be "better, happier, and safer" than our own.

Consider what happened to all the time that vanished with the avalanche of "time saving" electronic gadgets that have arrived since the mid-twentieth century. These devices were supposed to free us up to live more leisurely lives but now seem to strain our schedules. Yet we demand more and more, faster and faster— instant downloads, blistering news feeds, express mail, and rushed everything. We crave quick service, speedy gratification, split-second profits, and we want them now. Fast is never fast enough. We hate delays. We rage at long and sluggish checkouts, traffic bottlenecks, and software glitches. Amid our rage, patience has vanished, a casualty of our supersonic 5G world with all its crushing speed.

The late French scholar Paul Virilio saw speed—

intoxicating, recklessly accelerating speed—as *the* dom-
inant marker of hypermodernity. Daredevil velocity
leaves no time for deliberation or a measured response.
It triggers violence. And it kills.

Amish people stubbornly resist the breakneck speed
of hypermodernity. They demonstrate uncommon patience as they slowly make their way in our perilous
world. Their resistance to a speed-at-all-costs society
is shaped by their spiritual practices.

Their three-hour church service is a big slowdown.
The gathering offers no quick fixes for life's problems,
no stop-and-go religion, no instant gospel of prosper-
ity, no well-crafted mini-homily—just a slow-motion
service where everyone sits in a quiet patience that
hearkens back to a medieval monastery and reminds
the faithful that they are pilgrims plodding through
a high-speed world that's not their final home.

The worship service is also an incubator of patience
for children. No faith-formation classes by age groups
here, not even special classes for children. For hours,
young children sit quietly on wooden backless benches
or in a parent's lap. Midway through the service, a
small plate of crackers circulates as a snack for the
little ones. Children who tire of their father's lap may
toddle over to their mother's or aunt's. Most of the
time they sleep, sit quietly, or occupy themselves with
simple playthings—a small doll, a handkerchief, or tiny

bits of fabric or paper. Youngsters learn a big unspoken message: slowing down and listening is at the heart of Amish faith and identity. Being immersed in patience from infancy shapes their character and disposition for life.

Amish boys and girls can also be noisy and rambunctious, especially at play, yet they learn the yin and yang of fun and patience at an early age. Amish children don't race to the front of the food line. They wait patiently for their turn. Except for the very young, children at social gatherings eat after the adults have finished. With a half dozen or more siblings, children learn to wait for the bathroom, for a piece of pie, and for their chance to talk. Long before they're teens, they learn the lesson of patiently waiting.

Amish spirituality values the disciplines of waiting, of patience, of not rushing to conclusions, and of not forcing results. A father tells his teenage offspring that during *Rumspringa*, a time of greater freedom for adolescents, "I'll try to be patient with you, but I expect you to be patient with me too." Church leaders show patience to those who face sanctions for their trespasses by offering them time, weeks if necessary, to confess and amend their errors. Elders practice forbearance in other ways as well. Members who buy what was an English-owned home have a year to pull the plug on public grid electricity and convert to nonelectric lights, appliances, and heating systems that comply with church-community rules. Families with a member who requires access to an electrical medical device may tap into the public grid, if needed, for a specified length of time. When death strikes, the Amish greet the bereaved with "I wish you patience." Those same words bring comfort to a friend struggling with cancer or any other misfortune.

When faced with problems, the Amish default is to wait and pray, rather than seeking a quick fix. Indeed, the quick solution, the simple method, and the rapid cure that characterize our "instant" age are dangerous, declared one church leader. Demanding immediate solutions signals a lack of trust in God. Patience, for the Amish, is an enduring way of respecting each other and thoughtfully pondering options before rushing to foolish judgments.

Patience is a personal virtue, a social practice, and a spiritual stance. It's a way of living and a way of responding to whatever falls on our plate. Yes, it's an old-fashioned habit. But it's one that humanizes and moderates the speed of hypermodernity, one that allows time for deliberation and reflection, indeed one that may save us from violence. Amish ways remind us that many good things in life—slow-cooked food, emotional healing, forgiveness, and self-renewal—require time and patience to achieve their splendor.

❖

SIXTEEN

LIMITS

Less Choice, More Joy

Disturbed that outsiders sometimes think Amish people have no choices, Amos argued that they do indeed because the church doesn't control when to get married, whom to marry, where to live, where to work, what job to do, which flowers to plant, what to eat, or which hobbies to pursue. Amish people have many choices within a range of cultural boundaries. And they insist that fewer choices bring more joy.

Choice is woven into the fabric of modern life. We assume it's one of our inalienable rights. We think that more options—of pizza, cereal, blue jeans, swimsuits, cars, jobs, shows, phones, and a thousand other things—bring greater happiness. Comparing, selecting, and deciding make us happier, or so we think.

Even so, the speed by which new models pop up in

ads, fly off the shelves, and appear in showrooms leaves us exhausted. How many new styles of torn jeans can our brain process without overloading our circuits and sparking a migraine?

Psychologist Barry Schwartz, in *The Paradox of Choice: Why More Is Less*, found that while *some* choice is good, *more* choice isn't necessarily better. His work and that of others show that too many options inflict stress and diminish satisfaction with our final selection. We feel greater satisfaction, for instance, if we select an item out of three options rather than out of eleven.

Individuals bear the burden of choice in modern life, say the sociologists, whereas in small agrarian societies, tradition helps shoulder that burden. Similarly, Amish traditions reduce the weight of choice for members while still preserving ample options.

All of this affirms the Amish argument: fewer choices bring more joy.

❧

Choice was at the core of Amish origins in 1525. The Anabaptists founded a radical religion based on voluntary adult baptism that rejected no-choice infant christenings. The outrageous idea of choice in matters of faith and religion incurred the wrath of religious and civil authorities and triggered cruel persecution.

Amish churches still practice voluntary baptism. The

decision of young adults to accept baptism and join the
church is a choice to limit choice for the rest of their
lives. The much-romanticized practice of Rumspringa
begins when Amish youth turn sixteen and start spending weekends with their peers socializing and courting
at social gatherings. In this liminal time before baptism, they are between the authority of their parents
and the church. Upon baptism, at roughly eighteen
to twenty-two years of age, they become accountable
to the church. During Rumspringa, some youth may
decide not to affiliate with the Amish. Those who
choose to join the church—which on average is about
85 percent—then proceed to baptism.

At baptism, Amish novitiates bend their desires to
the dictates of the Ordnung: no cars, no public grid
electricity, no designer clothes, no computers, no televisions. Their baptismal vow implicitly prohibits higher
education, which blocks them from a host of occupations in the areas of law, science, medicine, politics,
and others.

-*-

Amish garb illustrates the paradox of choice. Two
religious values—*separation* from the world and *self-
denial*—regulate Amish wardrobes. In mainstream culture, dress articulates individuality. It's a tool of self-
adornment. It showcases individual taste, highlights
the body, and signals social status. While modern

dress accents the individual, Amish dress spotlights the group.

Amish people relinquish their right to self-expression and signal their commitment to communal authority when they don the garb of the church. Their clothing underscores group loyalty, not individual freedom and choice. Amish culture values humility, self-denial, deference to others, and *uffgevva*—giving up to the group. In Amish eyes, self-adornment—including cosmetics and jewelry—is a vain expression of pride, an abomination in the eyes of God.

At first glance, Amish people seem preoccupied with dress. Yet their conformity to prescribed dress standards frees them from incessant choice, from the burden of choice. They don't have to sort through their wardrobe in a frenzy each morning looking for matching outfits, nor do they spend endless hours shopping to stay abreast of fashion. So while Amish people may *appear* to be fixated on dress, they are liberated from it, spending much less time, money, and worry on clothing than most Americans do.

That said, women and girls spend a lot of time making clothing at home. And it's no small feat to keep a large family clothed. Yet the work is often shared, and simple clothing makes for swifter work.

In the larger society, about one in five American public schools requires uniforms. This practice relieves students of anxiety about their dress and, according to educators, promotes learning, equality, attendance, unity, and safety.

In modern culture, clothing fads, designer labels, and seasonal fashions encourage conformity to consumer styles. In this sense, both contemporary and Amish wardrobes reflect social compliance. Amish customs, however, are controlled by the church, not by fashion designers and clothing companies in faraway cities.

❋

Amish weddings also exemplify how tradition eases the burden of choice, especially for the bride and groom. No one needs a rehearsal because everyone knows the script. Tradition guides the protocol, which varies by community.

When a wedding approaches, everyone knows that it's never held on a Sunday. The brief ceremony comes at the end of a typical three-hour church service in a home, barn, or large building. Afterward, several hundred guests will enjoy a hot homemade meal with a stipulated menu. The afternoon festivities include much merrymaking, singing, snacks, and pranks, followed by an evening meal. In some communities, a prelude to the feast features an exciting parade of newly dating couples who may be prospects for the next wedding season.

Amid the tradition, there is some wiggle room for choice. The bride and groom may select the colors, but not the style, of their dress and that of their attendants. The couple may also decide to print their names on napkins and on thank-you cards for their gifts. These tiny personal touches pale in comparison with the many hours that modern couples often spend sorting through hundreds of options relating to the bridal party's dress, venue, liturgy, officiant, rehearsal, vows, celebratory aftermath, and honeymoon. Yet despite the many limits, Amish weddings are filled with fun and gaiety.

In all these ways, Amish tradition lifts the burden of choice from the shoulders of the bridal couple. No need for them to worry about making an "individual statement" that sets their wedding apart from others. Like a wedding planner, tradition reduces anxiety by managing the details of their special day.

Heeding the church's advice to restrict choices may seem constraining, but it brings the benefit of greater freedom. It's a rather simple formula: fewer choices reduce stress and invite more joy.

SEVENTEEN

·✳·

RITUALS

A Natural Detox

Nellie Bowles, a *New York Times* reporter, was on the phone. "I'm doing a story about the dopamine fasting fad in Silicon Valley," she said. In this kind of fasting, young people, mostly, were taking a time-out from technology inputs and other pleasurable stimuli. A kind of digital detox: No distractions, no stimuli, no tech. In its place, mindfulness, meditation, silence. "It reminds me," she said, "of some elements of Amish beliefs. Might that be the case?"

"Maybe," I replied.

The Amish have a mental fast of sorts built into their social rhythms, which swing back and forth between engage and pause, work and rest. While not the digital detox that Silicon Valley practices, Amish rituals do provide a periodic stepping-back from the tedium of work to regenerate psychological well-being.

Mini-rituals press the pause button several times a day. Long silent prayers open and close each meal. Family prayers, on bended knees, offer a benediction at day's end. These prayers insert moments of silence and reflection into daily life.

Sunday is a big respite from work. It's a day of worship, rest, and reverence. Work halts, except for the care of animals. Commercial transactions—buying anything, including groceries—cease. Amish businesses routinely post No Sunday Sales signs. People hire vehicles only for an urgent hospital visit or a distant funeral.

Congregations meet for services every other Sunday. On the Sundays they meet, the activities last about eight hours. The day begins early with horse-drawn travel, gathering time, a three-hour worship service, and a community meal with several seatings, followed by visiting into the afternoon. On "off" Sundays, a family may attend a neighboring service or spend a slow, quiet morning at home with an extended devotional, reading scripture and singing. The afternoon may include reading, visiting with friends, table or outdoor games, walking, hiking, and youth gatherings in the evening.

Yearly events also punctuate mundane life. An all-

day service for Holy Communion occurs each spring
and fall. A day or so before the service, people observe
a morning fast that involves skipping breakfast and
pausing from work for quiet meditation. There is also
a larger cycle of religious holidays celebrated by most
Amish communities: Second Christmas, Epiphany,
Easter Monday, Pentecost, Whit Monday (Pentecost
Monday), and Ascension Day. These special times encourage relaxing and visiting with extended family and
friends. This annual calendar organizes Amish life into
predictable rhythms of engagement and disengage-
ment, like the rising and falling of the tides.

Amish homes are remarkably quiet, but they are not
silent. People talk and tease, laugh and debate. What
makes them calm is the absence of most electric appliances: microwaves, air conditioners, hair dryers, and
vacuum cleaners. Absent also are video games, radios,
televisions, computers, paper shredders, digital timers,
and landline phones. And of course, no Alexa.

Business owners in some progressive groups may use
a landline, flip phone, or even a smartphone and computer at their worksite, which is typically not in the
home. These devices rarely enter the house and are
forbidden in more traditional groups. Having none
of the digital world on their person and none of it in
their house keeps digital clamor out of Amish homes,
leaving them quiet, apart from the whir of a sewing

machine, the hiss of gas lamps at night, the chime of a clock, or the sound of human voices. This calm offers a daily detox.

Silence offers a respite in other ways as well. An early eighteenth-century devotional booklet, still used in Amish circles, advises people "to avoid idle talk and let your speech be deliberate, a few words, and truthful. . . . It is [better to] remain silent than to say something which may be false or otherwise of no value." Amish people are comfortable with silence and feel no need to fill every pause in a conversation with words. Behavior expresses meaning better than words. A father who lost a daughter in the schoolhouse shooting at Nickel Mines said, "Our forgiveness was what we did, not what we said."

In many ways, Amish spirituality is quiet, remarkably so, compared with the noisy expressions of faith in some religious groups. For Amish people, God is best adored by patient waiting and solitude in a tumultuous world. A lengthy silent prayer, on bended knees, occurs in every church service. And silence is the final amen, the signature prayer at every burial in a simple cemetery in a grassy field.

Nature also provides a therapeutic pause. Although it's risky to make generalizations about Amish everywhere, I have never met an Amish person who didn't have a garden. Besides producing food for the family, gardens provide a restorative detox from the press and stress of life by connecting gardeners to the seasonal rhythms of planting and harvesting, the rising and setting of the sun, the last and first frost of the season— and also to the soil, the earthworms, and the mulch of organic life.

"Every child should have a creek wandering through their childhood," said one of my Amish bishop friends. Amish people believe that nature puts them in touch with God's handiwork and brings them into deep communion with God's divine spirit. It's a spiritual experience that's hard to explain to someone who's never planted seeds and witnessed them bear abundant fruit or never transplanted a flower and watched it flourish. One woman described the deep joy her flowers brought her with these words:

> I am strolling through my garden
> in the early morning dew.
> And I fill myself with happiness
> to last the whole day through.

With few digital devices to keep them indoors, Amish people spend the bulk of their leisure in nature. They enjoy ice-skating, hiking, camping, fishing, and hunting. They are avid birders. Nature, enthused one Amish person, is like a window into heaven.

In a society filled by verbosity and noise, silent time-outs can calm our mind and spirit. They're a salve for the 5G speeds of hypermodernity, with its around-the-clock shifts, always-open stores, and sleepless cyberspace. Time rushes on relentlessly, streaming forward, twenty-four seven, without moments of pause like the cyclical rhythms of Amish life. Time-outs, natural or digital, cleanse our bodies, temper our addictions, and refresh our souls.

EIGHTEEN

·❊·

RETIREMENT

Aging in Place

In *The Pursuit of Loneliness*, his best-selling 1970 book, Philip Slater argued that America's obsession with individualism was producing unhappy and lonely people. Dozens of other authors echoed that theme over the next fifty years with titles such as *Bowling Alone: The Collapse and Revival of American Community* (2000) and *Together: The Healing Power of Human Connection in a Sometimes Lonely World* (2020). With millions of clicks a day, the selfie generation documents the pervasive presence of individualism.

The rise of individualism was part of a broader social transformation. As individualism soared, family size declined, family members scattered across the continent in search of jobs, and more and more adults lived alone—28 percent by 2018. Loneliness was thriving, especially among older adults.

These demographic changes transformed how and where Americans retired. The old people's homes of the early twentieth century evolved into nursing homes and later into retirement villages and continuing care communities. These new patterns of aging separated family members by distance and function. For most children with older parents, the reality was even more complex. Increased financial inequality, rising costs, and stagnant incomes over the past fifty years significantly affected families' ability to provide care for their older members. Given these and other realities, some children were unable or lost the sense of duty to care for their elderly parents, leaving them to hire services or tap government coffers for their care.

Some twelve million Americans over age sixty-five live alone. Loneliness, especially among the elderly, has been called an epidemic by the American Psychological Association and the US Department of Health and Human Services. In 2018, worried about the uptick of loneliness in the United Kingdom, then prime minister Teresa May appointed a cabinet minister of loneliness because, "for far too many people, loneliness is the sad reality of modern life."

Social isolation and loneliness—exacerbated by living alone—is worse for one's health than smoking fifteen cigarettes a day and contributes to health hazards such as dementia, depression, anxiety, and heart disease. A plethora of research documents the harmful effects of social isolation and loneliness among the elderly.

Dozens of essays in AARP publications and online blogs with titles like "How to Stay Healthy while Aging" repeat a similar litany of suggestions: Stay active. Stay connected. Do things with friends. Make new friends. Exercise. Eat healthy food. Develop new hobbies.

Despite these developments in the broader society, the Amish remain committed to a communal way of life. They still spurn assertive individualism. Their families remain large. If they move to a new settlement, several families go together. And, as always, individuals never live alone.

Amish people rarely enter retirement centers or nursing homes. Their aging plan is simple: age in place. They didn't invent this practice. It's the way most rural Americans retired before 1950, long before the phrase became trendy. Indeed, even some non-Amish families still practice old-fashioned care at home or a modified version of it.

Amish people typically ease into retirement in their fifties. Aging in place for them means living in a "grandparent's apartment" annexed to the house of a son or daughter or in a bungalow on the same property. This arrangement enables the elderly to continue many of their lifelong activities, albeit at a slower pace. A grandmother might downsize a clothing or flower shop, work in a food store she previously owned before selling it to a daughter, or help with chores in the main house. Likewise, a grandfather might scale back his cabinet shop, work part-time in his son's construction company, help out with farm chores as needed, or start a small harness shop. As they age, some people begin new hobbies such as making toys or weaving rugs.

Aging in place means shifting roles but staying in the same social milieu of family, neighbors, and community. Apart from their own social activities, the aging person is immersed in the hubbub of the primary household's day-to-day events—visitors or business or farm activities—that offer continual surprises and stimulation. The family provides transportation for the retirees to church, community events, and family gatherings. Children and grandchildren also help them shop and coordinate medical appointments. As long as they are able, a retired couple may cook their meals and enjoy fresh produce from the family garden. Those who have lost their spouse may take some of their meals with their relatives next door in the main house. Amish aging in place requires a substantial investment of time and care from members of the extended family who live nearby.

One of the unique rewards of the Amish model is daily contact with some of their grandchildren and the joy of watching them mature. Grandchildren—with a poison ivy rash, hiccups, a stubbed toe, or a splinter in a finger—know where to run. Grandma knows, and she consoles.

In Amish society, the elderly are a respected source of wisdom. They are often consulted on the weather, on health problems that arise, or for advice about when to plant and harvest produce from the garden. Sometimes they're asked out of respect, but even so, it gives meaning to aging folks.

If a decline in health requires daily personal care, the adult children may take turns caring for a parent a week at a time or, depending on circumstances, may rotate the parent among their homes for several weeks at a time. Many elderly prefer to die at home, sometimes on the same property where they were born or lived after marriage.

When death approaches, the family knows the folklore, garnered over the ages, about death and dying. It holds the secrets about what to do and when to do it. Some change-minded Amish communities supplement the folk wisdom by turning to hospice care to reduce pain and provide comfort to the dying.

Aging in place for Amish people allows for a seamless transition into retirement with few disruptions. Family and friends—people they have known all their lives who love them and care for them—surround them in a setting similar to their childhood home. Aging in place may be old-fashioned, but it's smart, efficient, and healthy, not to mention modest in cost. Most important, this stay-at-home model effectively mitigates social isolation and loneliness.

·❊·

NINETEEN

FORGIVENESS

A Pathway to Healing

There they stood, late one afternoon on a crisp October day—a handful of bearded men in black—in the driveway of a modest home in Georgetown in southeastern Pennsylvania. An English man, a neighbor they knew well, stepped out of his house and walked toward them. One of them hugged him. Others shook his hand. Some cried. They talked for a few minutes. No one recalls the exact words spoken that day, but the body language said it all—so sorry, love you, no grudges, forgive you, don't move away—words of goodwill, grace, and mercy.

The English neighbor then turned and took those kind words back to his house and spilled them out to his daughter. Earlier that day, his daughter's husband, Charlie—a mile away at the one-room West Nickel

Mines School—had taken ten Amish girls hostage, bound their ankles, forced them to lie face down, and then shot them execution-style. Then he killed himself. Five girls would survive after receiving care in trauma centers. Five died.

At about the same time that the men arrived in the driveway, but unbeknownst to them, an Amish man visited a different home a few miles away. Charlie's father, Chuck Roberts, sat in shock, sobbing, with a towel around his head to soak up all his sweat and tears, on that dreadful day when every drop of hope had disappeared.

A retired police officer, Chuck often provided "taxi" service for his Amish neighbors. Suddenly, Henry, one of his clients, knocked on the door and walked in. "We call him our 'angel in black,'" said Terri, Charlie's mother. Her heart ached with that excruciating pain only a mother can know when she learns that her child has unleashed despicable violence on defenseless children.

No one saw his rage coming—not his parents, his pastor, his spouse, or his Amish neighbors. No one. In a note he left for his wife, he said he was angry at God for taking away their firstborn daughter who had lived for only twenty minutes after she was born nine years before. Now, on October 2, 2006, he had unloaded his rage by shooting ten of God's most innocent children.

For more than an hour, the angel in black consoled Chuck by repeating again and again, "Roberts, we love you. We love you." In Terri's words, "When Henry walked in the door, hope walked in the door."

The visits were spontaneous. The ambassadors had no script. No edict from the church. They were just doing the hard work of mending the neighborly fence between the Amish and the Roberts family.

Forgiveness was a "decided issue," an Amish bishop later told me. "We didn't need any meetings. It's just what Jesus taught us to do." It's the Amish default in the face of tragedy, a habit that runs deep in the Amish soul.

In some ways, the situation eased the hard work of forgiveness. The event ended as quickly as it had begun. Charlie was gone. The Roberts family and the Amish alike could only guess that a psychotic break had triggered the terrible shooting. Moreover, the Amish belief that vengeance is God's work gives them little energy to settle scores. They also hold a profound confidence that although God did not will the horrible schoolhouse shooting, God does sometimes transform such heinous acts into good. Charlie's bitterness, his inability to forgive God, was transfigured into a compelling story of forgiveness.

As word of the two visits gradually leaked out, their message flew worldwide with some twenty-four hundred media accounts featuring headlines like "Amish Forgive Man That Shot Their Children." The shocking story astounded most readers. Some pundits proclaimed that rushed forgiveness is unhealthy. Instant forgiveness is robotic and can be coerced they wrote. It overlooks the value of resentment and anger and downplays the social scorn that wickedness deserves. Besides, quick forgiveness implies that it's okay to walk into schools and slay innocent children.

Their swift response, Amish people said, was only the start of what would be a long journey. Several weeks later, one parent recalled, "When my son had a nightmare about the shooting, I had to start all over again with forgiveness." Forgiveness does not mask pain. Amish families shed puddles of tears. Instant forgiveness did not erase the anguish of losing a child or even two, as one family did.

Amid it all, one Amish man showed remarkable empathy. "The Roberts family had a much heavier burden to bear than we did," he said, speaking of all the shame and stigma piled on them by the horrific thing that one of their family members did to their Amish neighbors. And what of Charlie's eternal destiny? One Amish person expressed it this way: "I can only wish for him what I wish for myself: that God will be a gracious and merciful judge."

And what if Charlie had not died? "Well," said one

man, "if he were still living, he should be in jail so he wouldn't hurt other children." Would you visit him? "Of course we would," he said, drawing a sharp line between forgiveness and accountability.

And why did they forgive? They pointed to the Lord's Prayer: "forgive us our trespasses, as we forgive those who trespass against us" (Matthew 6:12). That's the prayer Amish people repeat silently before and after every meal, the prayer that closes every church service, and the first prayer a child learns to say. Forgiveness, one Amish leader reminded me, is the only idea that Jesus underscored at the end of the Lord's Prayer when he said, in essence, if you forgive, you will be forgiven. If you don't forgive, you won't be forgiven (Matthew 6:14–15). The same leader noted that Jesus implied, when he told his disciples to forgive more than seven times a day, that forgiveness should be a way of life.

It takes a lot of forgiveness to maintain harmony in a close-knit community. So central is the laying aside of grudges that Amish congregations have a kind of moral housecleaning. Two weeks before they celebrate Holy Communion each fall and spring, each church-community focuses on forgiveness, repairing broken relationships, and restoring unity. These engrained habits explain, in part, why forgiveness was their default response within hours of the tragedy.

Journalists who reached out to me asked, "Were the Amish prepared for this? Did their schools have emergency preparedness policies? Did they have emergency preparedness drills?" No, no, and no. Although the Amish schools scored zero on *emergency readiness*, they had *forgiveness preparedness*. In a world where the default is revenge, Amish forgiveness was ready to go when tragedy struck.

Despite such preparedness, forgiveness does not always come easy in a tightly knit community. Grudges and bitterness persist even in the hearts of people who know it's wrong. Even more egregious are the occasional times when Amish leaders urge victims of sexual abuse to forgive their perpetrators quickly or to live with abusive spouses because their religion requires it. When such wrongs are ignored or "forgiven" without expectations of accountability or repentance, it distorts relationships and suppresses the possibility of healing.

Amid these failures, the Amish commitment to forgiveness remains a distinctive trademark of their way of life in a broader culture that champions revenge. They understand how forgiveness can relieve those who are filled with grudges from the harms they have suffered. Amish people know that until they let go of bitterness, until they forgive, they will be tormented by the demons of the past, held hostage and controlled by an offender or an offense.

The psychological evidence is clear and abundant. Forgiveness, whether religiously motivated or not, is in our self-interest. It slows our pulse, lowers our blood pressure, and lessens anxiety and depression. It improves our immune system and self-esteem. Above all, it bolsters our mental health and provides an elixir for our well-being.

There's not a simple recipe for forgiveness. Each case is different. Doing it the Amish way or another way doesn't matter. What matters is taking the first step on a journey that promises to enhance our health and wholeness.

-❈-

They stand straight and tall. Five pear trees along a fencerow quietly face the sky, blending in with the seasons, unpretentious, without names or markers. Most who drive past them on that small country road speed by without noticing, but the locals know the secret. The Amish and their English neighbors all know that each somber tree testifies to a young life snatched out of this world on that tragic October day at the West Nickel Mines School, just thirty yards away.

·❋·

TWENTY

SUFFERING

A Higher Plan

The tragedy at Nickel Mines provoked discussions among Amish people about a perennial question: Why do bad things happen to good people? More specifically, why would God, who loves humanity, permit evil or even foreordain it? Or does God sit on the sidelines?

When asked after the shooting whether anyone in the church-community had asked how God could have let it happen, an Amish man responded, "Yes, probably a million times!" Yet allowing tragedy is not the same as directing it. A preacher at one of the funerals for the girls declared, "It's not God's will that people kill each other." An Amish mother agreed. "It wasn't God's will," she said. "God doesn't intervene and stop all the evil in the world. God doesn't stop people from making evil choices."

Although Amish people wrestle with questions of divine providence, they don't find easy answers. Nor do they have theological creeds that settle the thorny issues. "We must stop asking questions," said one person. "We will never have all the answers." "Every religion has mystery," said a craftsman. "I like to say a religion without mystery is like a wagon without wheels."

Even so, many expressed confidence that God doesn't make mistakes. God is in control. And this tragedy, like others, was somehow in God's long-range higher plan. One person voiced a broad sentiment when he said, "The shooting was in the Lord's hands. There is a higher power, and we simply need to bow down to it."

I asked Sadie, whose close friend Erma lost a daughter in the Nickel Mines shooting, "How do you pray for someone like Erma? And for people who are sick or hurt in an accident, do you say, 'I'm praying that God will heal you quickly'?"

"Oh no, we never say that or pray that," she said. "We don't ask God to do things for us. We always say, 'We wish you patience.' If a loved one dies or if someone has cancer, we always wish them patience to endure the suffering."

Explaining how he reacts to bad things, Amos said, "We often say *Gelassa*. It's a shortcut for *Gelassenheit*, a German word. Gelassa means 'Let it be. Just accept it. Don't fight back. Don't argue with God. Don't get angry with people who harm you. Just yield to it.'"

One woman explained Gelassenheit this way: "It's a yieldedness to whatever God sends. Especially an untimely death of a loved one or a long-term sickness but also the weather—drought, floods, extreme heat or cold, crop failure, missing the market, disease in animals, hail, fire." She concluded, "We don't pray for rain. We wait for rain, and when it comes, we thank God for it."

If nothing else, Amish people agree that the four words "Thy will be done" captures the meaning of yieldedness. It's the keystone of the Lord's Prayer that Jesus taught his disciples (Matthew 6:10). These words grace their minds in silent mealtime prayers, in spoken evening prayers, and at every worship service. The phrase headlines a collection of stories: *Thy Will Be Done: 134 Touching Personal Stories of Fatalities among Plain People.*

With their deep embrace of yieldedness, it's tempting to think that Amish people are mired in religious fatalism—a passivity that leaves them without agency or voice. But that's a wrong assumption. Yieldedness is only half the story.

⁂

Amish people act amid their suffering. They cope with it in two ways. First, they create Amish-style programs to support the needs of those who suffer and those who care for them. And second, they seek professional care in the outside world.

Some of their suffering arises from a small gene pool—the result of a small number of ancestral founders and few converts over the years. This combination produces a high incidence of genetic variants that cause disease. At the same time, a restricted gene pool provides a buffer from a few hereditary disorders found in the broader society.

✢

Amish people have always cared for their special-needs children. However, since 2000, a flurry of new programs has emerged. Parents established special schools and workshops for their "special sunbeams." Today, well over one hundred Amish special education schools operate across the country.

An annual special education conference for teachers and leaders of special schools and workshops began in 2000. Amish leaders at the gathering address topics such as Down syndrome, deafness, blindness, autism, seizures, attention-deficit/hyperactivity disorder, speech impairment, and dyslexia. In addition, special sunbeams (both children and adults) with a particular condition—blindness, multiple sclerosis, autism, and so on—attend annual "reunions" with their families for information and support.

In 2006, two special education teachers founded the magazine *Life's Special Sunbeams*. Stories—written by parents of special children, their teachers, and special-needs adults—fill the pages of this monthly periodical. In one story, an adult paralyzed by polio in both legs and her right arm explains her morning routine of rising from bed. She performs a series of fifty-five sequential moves to get into a sitting position and maneuver from the bed to her wheelchair. Seven minutes was her best time ever. The poignant stories educate parents, teachers, and sunbeams and remind everyone that they are part of a larger family struggling with similar issues.

Christian G. Esh, an Amish education leader, recalls that before the 1980s, children with special needs "were called 'retarded' and treated that way. Now, we call them 'special.'" For him, that shift in language changed people's views and greatly improved the lives of many families with special-needs members.

⁜

In 1989, a peculiar thing happened near the town of Strasburg in eastern Pennsylvania. A young doctor quietly started making house calls to the homes of Plain people. He focused on children with unique diseases caused by genetic variants among the Plain people that had never been diagnosed or treated. The young physician listened carefully to the painful stories these families told about the suffering of their children.

The doctor was a stranger. He had graduated from Harvard and conducted research at big-city universities. So it was remarkable that he showed genuine interest in the lives of Plain people and asked questions about their diet, daily habits, and church. The story is also remarkable because Plain people—who had never studied any science, who associated it with evolution, who lived separatist lives, who put more faith in medicinal folklore than in modern medicine, and who didn't trust worldly people and their ways—were willing to confide in and trust this strange doctor.

Even though the parents believed that the afflictions were part of the divine plan, they wanted to do something, anything, to help relieve the suffering of their dearly beloved children. They needed a balm, some hope. So they helped construct a building, a clinic for the doctor, in an Amish cornfield south of Strasburg.

The story is also remarkable because Dr. D. Holmes Morton and the staff who joined him at the Clinic for Special Children dared to rethink medicine. They boldly adapted it to fit Plain community culture. They *culturalized* modern medicine by aligning it with the needs and sensibilities of Plain people.

The cornfield experiment prospered. Today it serves patients from around the world. Since its beginning in

1990, the clinic has served 4,700 patients, both Plain and English, from forty-two states and seventeen countries. In a recent year, the clinic had 1,091 active patients and some 1,700 patient visits, managed 382 known genetic variants that cause disease, and identified 76 new disease-causing genetic variants.

The clinic seeks to integrate advanced scientific research with clinical care. This formula provides Plain people and others—born with genetic predispositions to disability, chronic disease, or death—access to timely, affordable, and effective health care. The clinic's mission draws young doctors and scientists who are eager to explore cutting-edge advances in genome medicine.

Happily, a half dozen similar clinics have emerged to serve Plain people in other states. The people's warm acceptance of the clinics demonstrates how the Amish and other Plain people are willing to blend scientific advances in genetics with their traditional views of suffering and divine providence.

TWENTY ONE

NONRESISTANCE

No Pushback

It was an ugly stain of sin on the Amish heart. Not out there in the English world. Not in big-city gangs. Not in political corruption. But at the core of the Amish soul—deceit, malice, incest, sexual assault, and the abuse of women and men who defied a cultlike religious leader answering to no one but himself. It was an aberration of Amish life. Such moral rot in a church-community was unknown in Amish history. Over the ages, the bishops had warned of the terrible things that occur when a self-willed person disobeys the collective counsel of the church.

Bishop Samuel Mullet declared that he was a prophet who spoke for God. He cited war in the Bible to endorse force and dismiss the nonviolent teachings of Jesus. Mullet openly defied the counsel of three hundred elders who unanimously condemned his behavior. He then retaliated by launching a series of late-night beard-cutting attacks against selected leaders and other critics in several counties in Ohio in 2011.

Mullet and sixteen co-conspirators were eventually charged with, among other things, federal hate crimes against Amish people. That the peace-and-forgiveness-loving Amish were the first group in America to be charged with intragroup hate crimes just boggled the minds and dropped the jaws of Amish and English alike. The publicity shamed Amish people everywhere. The disgrace went viral, reaching every Amish hamlet from Pennsylvania to Montana, Michigan to Texas. The news stories proliferated, covering the initial attacks, the investigation, the FBI raid, the three-week trial in Cleveland, and finally the sentencing in 2013.

❄

I agreed to serve as an expert witness in the federal trial in September 2012. In preparation, I stayed with Bishop Raymond Hershberger and his wife, Sara, one evening in their home in Ohio. We talked into the night about how the attackers broke in and pulled him out of bed and cut off his beard, causing him so much shame that he didn't preach in church for six months. We talked about the upcoming trial. The federal prosecutors wanted Raymond to testify because he was the most senior bishop of all the victims. Should he refuse, they might subpoena him.

If ever there were a time for revenge, this was it. If ever there were a moment to justify retaliating against Bishop Mullet for how his awful behavior hurt and sullied Amish people everywhere, this was it. But payback isn't the Amish way.

Raymond told me that even testifying against someone in court was using force, was saying things that might condemn the person. Testifying was resistance to evil, the opposite of what Jesus taught us. Jesus said that we shouldn't resist evil. He taught us to love our enemies, to pray for those who persecute us (Matthew 5:39–44). Then, Raymond reflected, "I only got a haircut. Why should I push back? Look at Jesus. He didn't fight back when he was tortured. He even asked God to forgive his tormentors as he bled on the cross."

The bishop then recalled his Anabaptist forebears in Europe in the sixteenth century and talked about how they weren't defiant. How they didn't fight back. Just like Jesus, the early Anabaptists had offered radical forgiveness to their executioners who kindled fires to burn them at stakes. Others, moments before they were beheaded or drowned in lakes, also expressed forgiveness. Look at all those pictures and stories in our big *Martyrs Mirror*, suggested Raymond, referencing the 1660 volume that records the persecution of Anabaptist martyrs. Raymond had preached nonresistance in his sermons for many years. Year after year, he had taught it to young adults in catechism classes. For him now to use the worldly court to get back at Bishop Mullet—why that would be plain hypocrisy.

Still, some of Raymond's fellow bishops suggested a different way to think about it. "Couldn't you tell the truth," they asked him, "just tell the truth about what happened that night when they broke in and dragged you out of bed?" Just be a witness to the truth. That seemed different from fighting back.

Later on, after much prayer and soul-searching, Raymond finally agreed to testify to the truth, partially because he worried that if Bishop Mullet were not stopped, he would keep on hurting people.

✢

Nonresistance is the bedrock of the Amish moral order. It does not focus on social justice or trying to stop evil. It doesn't join nonviolent protests. Nonresistance, in short, is just radical, no payback forgiveness. If you believe, as the Amish do, that vengeance is God's responsibility, then you don't need to shoulder the burden of retaliation (Romans 12:19).

Nonresistant convictions have led Amish people to reject military service. These beliefs also undergird the ban on litigation, another type of force. Amish people do not hold public office because the legal obligations of holding office might require that they engage in litigation or use force to protect public safety.

Nonresistance also guides aspects of daily life. Silence, rather than a boisterous retort or argument, is the Amish default amid conflict. When perplexed by an attorney or a bureaucrat, outwitted by a regulation, or cursed by an outsider, the Amish response is often silence.

Still, some acts blur the line between resistance and nonresistance. Is the use of pepper spray acceptable for self-defense—or is that a form of resistance? Several well-respected bishops in Ohio reportedly carried pepper spray to protect themselves from Bishop Mullet's militia. After the Nickel Mines tragedy, discussions percolated about providing pepper spray to women teaching in Amish schools. Opinions on pepper spray vary widely.

Nonresistance is the ultimate yieldedness to God's will. It's also the ultimate submission of the self. A nonresistant act proclaims that there's a bigger truth than one's life. Unlike soldiers who die for the cause of nationalism, the nonresistant soul—standing without weapons or threat of revenge, and with forgiveness for the foe—points to the bigger, the higher truth of God's nonviolent ways.

The fearlessness of nonresistance is utterly counter-cultural. It defies all our natural and social impulses. Still, its everlasting light burns bright in a hate-filled world.

TWENTY TWO

DEATH

A Good Farewell

When an Amish person's life dwindles and nears its end, something remarkable happens in some of the more progressive Amish communities. The English arrive. They are welcomed into the most private domain of Amish life, the home. Hospice staff assist members of the extended family, who rotate as caregivers for their ailing kin. Family members trust the hospice staff to provide palliative care and comfort as their loved one fades away.

Amish funerals are preplanned without charge, courtesy of tradition. There is only one way to commemorate a death in Amish country when the word leaks out that a soul has departed for heaven. Custom sets off a host of activities that help shoulder the burden for the grieving family. The template varies a bit here and there across the country, but everyone knows the ritual for their own church-community.

Friends immediately take over the chores of the surviving family. Other friends begin buying and preparing food for the standard funeral menu, and still others supervise the seating arrangements for three to four hundred people and the plans to park carriages and stable dozens of horses and other tasks.

Everyone knows the ritual; knows the undertaker; knows that the embalmed body (without makeup) will be returned to the home, where the family will dress it in traditional apparel and place it in a simple hardwood coffin; and knows that the body will remain in the home for two days as members of the community, often in the hundreds, drop in with food and quiet words of solace and then sit in silence to show their support for the bereaved.

Everyone knows—the moment the soul takes flight— which scriptures and prayers will be read in the simple hour-and-a-half-long funeral service; knows that a large black hearse pulled by horses will lead the long snakelike procession of carriages to the cemetery, where the body will soon return to Mother Earth from where it came; knows that after a brief scripture reading, silent prayers will be offered; and knows that the deceased one's headstone will be identical in size and style to all the other headstones set in rows in the fenced-in cemetery surrounded by pasture. As the long train of carriages heads back to the house for the communal meal, the rhythmic clip-clop of the horseshoes on the country road reminds everyone that life's journey goes on.

Everyone knows all of this. Knows the routine by heart.

These rituals were especially comforting to a friend of mine. With tears of appreciation, he warmly recounted the communal meal after his wife's burial. And then asked rhetorically, "Where else could you ever get support like that?" For him, the answer was *nowhere*, nowhere else.

No search for a funeral director is necessary in Amish country. No discussions about cremation versus burial or about the cost of the funeral or about the style of the casket or about a memorial service versus a funeral or about the funeral program and the music— not one of these happens. None. Tradition settled them long ago.

In the days after a funeral, Amish practices continue to offer emotional support to those who are grieving. Families who have lost a loved one will typically receive Sunday afternoon and evening visits from friends for several months or even up to a year. The guests may sit in silence or engage in hushed conversations while grieving family members recount stories of the departed.

Members of a grieving family typically receive cards in the months after a death. In one case, a family who lost a child received hundreds of notes from friends across the country. Families who lose a loved one by sudden death—drowning or accident or other unforeseen event—are welcome to join the "Sudden Death" circle letter that circulates among others who share a similar loss and to attend the annual Sudden Death Reunion for encouragement as well.

After the death of a spouse, parent, sibling, or child, bereaved women show they are in mourning by wearing a black dress in public settings for several months or longer. The length of time depends on the bereaved's relationship with the person who died. This mourning ritual allows others, even those that don't know the woman well or know of her loss, to ask thoughtful questions that open the door for conversation.

The tears flow, but the sobs are restrained, as people submit quietly to divine purpose. From cradle to grave, the mysteries of life and death unfold in the context of loving families and supportive rituals. An English funeral director thoughtfully observed that these well-established rituals enable Amish people to accept death in graceful ways.

The rites of farewell in Amish society embody many

of their enduring values. The funeral demonstrates their commitment to simplicity, equality, community, and separation from the English world. The simple ritual enactments, without flowers or elaborate caskets, are held in a barn, home, or shop but never in a funeral home or a church. These customs downplay individuality, personal achievement, status, and wealth. Eulogies are absent. All praise goes to God, not to the deceased. Everyone enters the eternal community on equal footing. No large memorial stones or sculpted monuments signify social status or wealth after the burial.

Like a sturdy handrail along a dark path in the shadow of death, tradition lifts the anxieties of decision-making from the shoulders of the bereaved and enables them to ponder deeply the words of a well-known hymn that they have sung since childhood:

Consider, man! The end,
Consider your death,
Death often comes quickly;
He who today is vigorous and ruddy,
May tomorrow or sooner,
Have passed away.

NEGOTIATION
NEVER ENDS

In the first essay, I explained how the Amish negotiate with modernity by scrutinizing new developments to see whether they have the potential to weaken or strengthen their community. This epilogue returns to that theme by recounting their century-long struggle with the telephone—a struggle that recently intensified over smartphones. This fascinating story reminds us that negotiating is an ongoing process.

The riddles of Amish culture—practices that seem incongruent if not hypocritical to outsiders—stirred my initial interest in Amish studies. As I delved into Amish society, the idea of negotiating with modernity helped me grasp the cultural logic underlying the perplexing puzzles of their way of life. I learned that Amish people *accepted* certain practices (gas barbecue grills), *rejected* others (television), and *bargained* with still others.

The riddle of motor vehicles exemplifies a bargain. Amish leaders forbade car ownership but permitted members to hire rides in motor vehicles owned and operated by outsiders. This bargain kept cars from fragmenting church-communities while, at the same time, tapped some of the benefits of high-speed travel. Beneath each riddle is a negotiated bargain, so to speak, that keeps threats at arm's length while still granting access to new cultural developments.

These cultural puzzles that piqued my curiosity in Amish life still fascinate me today. Amish creativity in negotiating with modernity has enabled them not only to survive but to thrive in our hyper-everything world.

All the while, Amish life keeps changing, as does the rest of society. Some scholars have traced a shift in contemporary culture in recent years. In their view, the solid forms of modern life in the late nineteenth and early twentieth centuries brought stability through their slow-to-change social customs, bureaucratic institutions, and industrial factories. But in the last quarter of the twentieth century, some of those *solid* forms began to melt into *liquid* ones.

You can see this in the shift from still photos to video, from landline to mobile phones, from a manufacturing economy to one that cranks out information and services, from store-based commerce to internet sales, from physical books to e-books, and from tanks to cyber warfare. One Amish writer described the melting this way: "Modern society is a great big melting pot. Everything that goes into the pot gets melted down, stirred together and mixed up." The World Wide Web shows the amorphous, fleeting, ever-changing liquid forms of twenty-first-century culture. Everything becomes foggy, fuzzy, and flaky. We don't know whom or what to trust.

Throughout the twentieth century, the Amish resisted solid forms of modern technology—phones, cars, tractors, public grid electricity, chilling tanks for milk, television, and computers—that threatened their way of life. Amish church-communities discussed, sometimes for years, the good and the bad of new devices. And eventually, they decided their fate.

Leaders could easily enforce taboos on big technologies. Anyone could see public electric lines attached to a house or a tractor in a field, for instance. Even personal computers in their early days were a big box sitting on a desk.

The transformation from solid to liquid modernity, however, overturned some of the earlier bargains. The best example of this is the endless revisions to telephone bargains.

-❖-

The phone has a long and complicated history in Amish society. Even after twelve decades of having access to the technology, church-communities across the country vary widely in their stance on phones. The phone was the first technological device to distinguish the Amish from their English neighbors. Ever since then, technology—or restrictions on it—has marked Amish identity.

Around 1905, a few people installed primitive party-line phones in their homes. The party lines included nearby English and Amish patrons. Anyone could listen in on a party-line call. Party lines understandably raised eyebrows because they linked the outside world to private Amish homes that provided refuge from the outside world and that also served as a place of worship. Homes were the most sacred place in Amish society. Amish and English callers alike could suddenly disrupt family routines. Worse yet, they could listen in on private conversations. The phone also threatened face-to-face visiting. If you could call, why visit?

It's not surprising that leaders asked families to tear out their phones. Still, access to a phone was handy for emergencies such as a fire or a sick child. Thus, some church-communities allowed members to place calls from a public phone booth or an English neighbor's home. This agreement was the first riddle in Amish history to distinguish *ownership* of technology from *access* to it.

The phone's century-long probation spurred dozens of controversies in church-communities around many questions: Should we permit the use of public phones? What about using an English neighbor's phone? Might phones be housed in a shanty (shed) at the end of the lane for outgoing calls only? Should families share a neighborhood phone? How close may a phone be to the house? May one be installed inside a business, or must it remain outside in a phone shanty? What about in a barn or other outbuilding on Amish property?

One Amish man told me in the 1980s, "If you have a place of business and need a phone, it must be *separate* from the shop, and if it's on the farm, it must be *separate* from the house. It should be *shared* with the community so that others can use it. It's just not allowed in the house—where would it stop? We stress keeping things small and keeping the family together."

Amish people had a good grasp of how a phone would disturb family life with interruptions, would spoil the flow of family rhythms and mealtime prayers, and would allow unwanted visitors into a home at any moment. So over the years, hundreds of church-communities across North America negotiated and renegotiated telephone bargains to protect family life

from outside interference. These ever-changing bargains created a series of riddles. Nonetheless, the phone
kept inching closer and closer to the home. By the
mid-1980s, after eight decades of debate, one exasper-
ated grandmother declared, "The phone is still on
probation!"

✤

In the twentieth century, Amish people had built the
software, so to speak, to cope with solid technology,
but they had little in their cultural toolbox for dealing
with the flood of liquid technology.

In the mid-1990s, a few early adopters in progress-
minded communities quietly began using mobile flip
phones to test the waters. The mobiles were different
from anything Amish people had ever faced. They
were small. You could hide and silence them. They
were portable and not attached to the home. And the
mobiles were private—controlled by individuals, not
church-communities—at least not until they became
a public issue.

The mobiles caught church leaders off guard because they were easy to hide. A businessman who kept
one in the top drawer of his office desk told me with a
mischievous smile in the late 1990s, "The ministers will
never be able to stop them now. There's just too many.
They have no idea how many people have them."

Mobiles were handy for contractors and market-stand owners. Contractors used them to coordinate jobs and work crews. Stand owners who traveled weekly to dozens of farmers' markets on the Eastern Seaboard depended on them to order products and to stay connected to family back home. Some church-communities eventually made special rules for businesspeople: Keep your mobile in the truck, shop, or office. Never bring it into the house.

Mobile phones proved to be less vexing than the smartphones that followed. The smarties began slipping into change-minded communities about 2010. They sparked controversy by challenging two fundamental tenets of Amish faith—separation from the world and communalism.

For centuries, Amish people were taught not to love the world, to distance themselves from it, and to avoid all appearances of worldliness. Separation from the world guided church decisions about dress regulations, technology guidelines, and involvements in secular society.

Smarties suddenly put the whole world in Amish hands. They felled the boundaries of separation by channeling unfiltered worldliness through a handheld gadget. Smarties leapfrogged an entire century of discussions about keeping the phone out of homes. They mocked all the fervent admonitions of church leaders against using televisions, computers, cameras, recorders, and videos by packing all of them into one small device. One Amish man explained, "The smartphone is just overwhelming. It's overstimulating. You have all the stimulus. You have visual, you have auditory, you have it all." Unlike mobiles, those features made smarties addictive.

In previous essays, I underscored the communal foundations of Amish life—the give and take of decision-making, the long process of collective discernment, and the importance of yielding to churchly authority. Assertive individualism disrupts all of that and threatens the harmony and stability of church-communities. Now with a tap on their smarty, individuals can dabble in a multitude of ideas that contradict Amish faith and life. Absorbing dissident views without any input from their church-community can embolden individuals to question church authority.

An educational gathering for several dozen Rumspringa-age youth in a change-minded settlement illustrates the shift toward individual authority. The adult leaders at the gathering counseled the sixteen- to twenty-year-olds to "be careful about what you see on your phones and make good decisions about immoral things." This advice rested on two assumptions: young people had smarties, and they were responsible enough to decide how to use them.

Throughout the twentieth century church-commu-

nities vetted new technology and made *collective* decisions about its use. For example, in the 1930s and
1940s, the vast majority of Amish church-communities
prohibited farmers from using tractors to till, culti-
vate, and harvest crops. That prohibition remains in
effect today. Yet *individual* youth are given the freedom in some church-communities to determine their
use of smarties. Giving teenagers such discretion arguably breaches separation from the world far more than
any tractor could.

A young businessman who owns a smarty worries
more about the breakdown of communal ties than
about breaching separation from the world. "I'm not
as worried about pornography," he explained, "as I
am about seeing boys at social gatherings just staring
at their phones instead of chatting together."

For some members of church-communities, smarties offer a portal into an exciting new world; for
others, they are a deadly weapon for the Amish way of
life. Amish responses to smarties fall into the typical
categories of negotiation: rejection, acceptance, and
bargaining.

The *rejecters* spurn smarties. But without a pope
or a central church body, it's impossible to ban them
broadly by fiat when final church authority rests in each
of the twenty-six hundred Amish church-communities
in North America. Some clusters of congregations

have joined together to stop smarties. These churches ask youth at baptism if they have a smarty. Those who have one must purge it before they can join the church. Such church-communities also excommunicate members who have one if they refuse to discard it. Many rejecters hold fast to the older practice of allowing landline phones in shanties on Amish property as long as the phone remains outside the house. The ultra-traditional affiliations still forbid owning any phone. One may only borrow an English neighbor's phone for a few minutes or ask the neighbor to place a call.

On the other end of the spectrum stand the *acceptors*, at least by default. Although few, if any, of the progress-minded church-communities officially approve smarties, they tolerate them, thus allowing them de facto. In large progress-minded settlements with dozens of church-communities, some accept smarties while others do not. A businessman in a sizable settlement estimated that "one-third of the bishops don't say much about them, another third preach against them but don't enforce it, and the final third will excommunicate you if you have one."

Finally, the *bargainers* have created new arrangements to access phones without permitting smarties. Some smarty-resistant church-communities permit Jitterbug-style mobiles with voice only or with voice and text only. Another popular bargain in smarty-

resisting churches allows for so-called black-box mobiles provided by a Verizon Wireless Home Phone connection. None of the mobile options, however, has a camera, video games, or online access.

An ex-Amish man who serves many Amish customers at his farm supply store in a change-minded settlement saw no turning back: "Smartphones will change Amish life forever!" An Amish leader looking to the future observed, "We already have many different ways to connect to online stuff without a smarty. It's like a game of whack-a-mole. You whack out one, and three more pop up! Who knows what else will emerge." In a world awash with liquid modernity, one thing is certain: successful negotiations will require a lot of agility.

-❊-

The final lesson for all of us is this: Negotiation empowers individuals and communities. It encourages us to be fearless—to have the courage to buck the powerful tides of modernity; to refute the pervasive assumption that bigger, faster, and newer are always better; and to reject the enticing narrative that individuals are smart enough to chart their odyssey alone.

Successful negotiation requires a community, a village to sort and screen the options. Yet negotiating culture, and deciding what to accept, reject, and transform, takes work that never ends. And to do that work, we need one another and our collective wisdom.

ACKNOWLEDGMENTS

This book rests on a bedrock of kindness extended to me by dozens of Amish people who generously shared their time and ideas. I thank them for their gracious spirit and cherish their friendship. Two examples of their hospitality and welcome are memorable.

On one occasion, a bishop friend in Ohio invited me to stay overnight in his home during a research trip. I left him a phone message saying that I would likely arrive at about eight o'clock at night. He responded with a phone message saying, "We probably won't get home until eleven o'clock. We'll leave the lantern in the kitchen turned low. Just come in and make yourself at home and go to bed. Don't worry about the dog; he's old and lazy, and he'll be happy to see you."

Late one Saturday in February, I drove to a home in central Pennsylvania to visit friends who had invited me to their church. After traveling on ice-covered back roads, I was anxious about finding their house in the dark. It's always daunting to arrive at an Amish home in darkness with no outdoor electric lights. Happily, when I got near their home, I saw a lantern hanging on the post at the front of their house. It provided me light for navigating the icy steps up to their porch.

Throughout my Amish research, I have enjoyed collaborating with wonderful colleagues. I coauthored Amish-themed books with Carl Desportes Bowman, Karen M. Johnson-Weiner, Steven M. Nolt, and David L. Weaver-Zercher, among others. In the coauthored books, each author contributed to and revised all of the chapters, making it difficult to know which person provided a particular idea. I plead forbearance for any ideas that I may have inadvertently borrowed from my colleagues.

Conversations with James A. Cates, Sally Esh, Anna Mary Fisher, Linda King, David King, David Kline, Steven M. Nolt, Ben Riehl, Terri Roberts, Judy Stavisky, and Wayne Wengerd have enriched my understanding of some of the topics in this book. I'm grateful for their insights and contributions to these essays.

Over the years, I have been fortunate to have an academic home at the Young Center for Anabaptist and Pietist Studies of Elizabethtown College. It's an intellectually stimulating setting for research and writing. I treasure the warm support of my colleagues Jeff Bach, Edsel Burdge Jr., Hillary Daecher, David Eller, Cynthia Nolt, Steven M. Nolt, Stephen Scott, and Brenda Spiker. They have a knack for turning work into fun. Thanks to all of you.

I also acknowledge the peer reviewers solicited by Johns Hopkins University Press for their constructive feedback on an early draft of the manuscript. I'm incredibly grateful to Sara Versluis, whose deft editorial skills enhanced the narrative's clarity and flow.

It's always a pleasure to work with the wonderful people at JHU Press. I'm grateful beyond measure for the keen advice and unwavering support of Gregory M. Britton, editorial director, and his superb team. They know how to infuse publishing with a spirit of delight. Accolades to all of them.

NOTES

Preface: When Old Is New Again

viii *Amish-wannabe books like*: Nancy Sleeth, *Almost Amish: One Woman's Quest for a Slower, Simpler, More Sustainable Life* (Chicago: Tyndale House, 2012).

ix *For example, the 2017 post-apocalyptic novel*: David Williams, *When the English Fall: A Novel* (Chapel Hill, NC: Algonquin Books, 2018).

xi *Doubling every twenty years*: The Young Center's Amish Studies website provides resources on Amish culture and population statistics, http://groups.etown.edu/amishstudies/.

Essay 1. Riddles: Negotiating with Modernity

2 *The controversy surrounding the film*: See John A. Hostetler and Donald B. Kraybill, "Hollywood Markets the Amish," in *Image Ethics: The Moral Rights of Subjects in Photographs, Film, and Television*, ed. Larry Gross, John Stuart Katz, and Jay Ruby (New York: Oxford University Press, 1988), 220–35.

3 *The Amish were, I thought, negotiating with modernity*: I first used this conceptual paradigm in the first edition of Donald B. Kraybill, *The Riddle of Amish Culture* (Baltimore: Johns Hopkins University Press, 1989). The paradigm in my current understanding appears in Donald B. Kraybill, "Response: How Do We Know What We Know about the Amish and

Other Minorities?," *Journal for the Scientific Study of Religion* 58, no. 3 (2019): 743–52.

Essay 2. Villages: Webs of Well-Being

7   *As I wrapped up a discussion*: Chelsea Marcantel, *Everything Is Wonderful* (New York: Samuel French).

7   *Contented people may live in villages*: Arun Abey, "The Most Contented People on Earth, But Are They the Happiest?" Arun Abey: Decisions for Wealth and Wellbeing (blog), December 8, 2013, https://www.arunabey.com/happiness-wellbeing/the -most-content-people-on-earth-but-are-they-the-happiest/.

7   *We also know that robust social ties*: Vivek H. Murthy, *Together: The Healing Power of Human Connection in a Sometimes Lonely World* (New York: HarperCollins, 2020).

11   *Leaders urge members to*: *1001 Questions and Answers on the Christian Life* (Aylmer, ON: Pathway, 1992), 158.

13   *The national "weaver" movement*: Weave: The Social Fabric Project, sponsored by the Aspen Institute, https://weare weavers.org/.

13   New York Times *columnist David Brooks*: David Brooks, "A Nation of Weavers," op-ed, *New York Times*, February 18, 2019, https://www.nytimes.com/2019/02/18/opinion/culture -compassion.html.

Essay 3. Community: Taming the Big "I"

17   *The pact is countercultural*: For background, consult Donald B. Kraybill, *The Riddle of Amish Culture*, rev. ed. (Baltimore: Johns Hopkins University Press, 2001), 33–36; Donald B. Kraybill, Karen M. Johnson-Weiner, and Steven M. Nolt, *The Amish* (Baltimore: Johns Hopkins University Press, 2013), 100–2.

18   *The title of an Amish essay*: "The Big 'I,'" *Family Life*, August–September 2007, 6–8.

18 *For Amish people, self-denial means*: 1001 *Questions*, 76–77.

19 *One Amish publication puts it starkly*: 1001 *Questions*, 125.

Essay 4. Smallness: Bigness Ruins Everything

23 *From egos to social units*: See Kraybill, *Riddle of Amish Culture*, rev. ed., 106–10; and Kraybill, Johnson-Weiner, and Nolt, *The Amish*, 171–74.

25 *In such a thick-context culture*: This is more commonly called "high-context culture." See Edward T. Hall, *Beyond Culture* (New York: Anchor Books, 1977).

27 *To address the problem*: See Marc A. Olshan, "The National Amish Steering Committee," in Donald B. Kraybill, ed., *The Amish and the State*, 2nd ed. (Baltimore: Johns Hopkins University Press, 2003), 66–84.

Essay 5. Tolerance: A Light on a Hill

29 *For the Jewish scholar*: Yuval Noah Harari, *21 Lessons for the 21st Century* (New York: Penguin Random House, 2019), 196–98.

29 *Fifty-year-old Rebecca*: Kraybill, *Riddle of Amish Culture* (1989).

34 *Amish writer Benuel Blank put*: Benuel S. Blank, "Being a Witness to Tourists," in *The Scriptures Have the Answers* (Parkesburg, PA: Blank Family, 2009), 154.

Essay 6. Spirituality: A Back Road to Heaven

37 *With some exceptions, the Old Order Amish*: For exceptions see Steven M. Nolt, "The Amish 'Mission Movement' and the Reformulation of Amish Identity in the Twentieth Century," *Mennonite Quarterly Review* 75, no. 1 (2001): 7–36.

37 *Amish writer Benuel Blank writes*: Benuel S. Blank, "The Ausbund Songwriters on the Assurance of Salvation," in *The Amazing Story of the Ausbund* (Narvon, PA: Benuel S. Blank, 2001), 105–8.

37 *Amish spirituality is couched*: See Kraybill, *Riddle of Amish*

Culture, rev. ed., 36–38; Kraybill, Nolt, and Weaver-Zercher, *Amish Grace*, 100–2, 167–69; Kraybill, Johnson-Weiner, and Nolt, *The Amish*, 70–72.

39 *In some ways, evangelical and Amish vocabularies*: This analogy comes from Gary Chapman, *The Five Love Languages: How to Express Heartfelt Commitment to Your Mate* (Chicago: Northfield, 2004).

39 *An admonition in one of their devotional books*: "Rules of a Godly Life," in *In Meiner Jugend: A Devotional Reader in German and English*, trans. Joseph Stoll (Aylmer, ON: Pathway, 2000), 103.

Essay 7. Family: A Deep and Durable Bond

43 *Amish families are large*: Kraybill, Johnson-Weiner, and Nolt, *The Amish*, 193–211.

45 *Aaron Beiler called me one evening*: Aaron F. Beiler, *Light in the Shadow of Death* (New Holland, PA: Aaron F. Beiler, 2008).

Essay 9. Parenting: Raising Sturdy Children

53 *In recent years some baby boomers*: Hannah Fry, "Back to Basics: Universities Are Now Offering 'Adulting' Classes," *Star Tribune*, last modified January 7, 2020, https://emsglobal.me /usa-back-to-basics-universities-are-now-offering-adulting -classes/; Stephan Bisaha, "Colleges Teach Students the Basics of 'Adulting,'" last modified December 9, 2019, https://www .wbur.org/hereandnow/2019/12/09/how-to-be-an-adult.

54 *Amish leaders and writers consistently emphasize*: See Kraybill, *Riddle of Amish Culture*, rev. ed., 33–39; Kraybill, Johnson-Weiner, and Nolt, *The Amish*, 193–211; Kraybill, Nolt, and Weaver-Zercher, *Amish Way*, 93–105.

54 *A widely cited poem in Amish circles*: "Die Kinder Zucht," *Grapevine*, April 2, 2008, 6. English translation by Walton Z. Moyer.

55 *So it's not surprising*: *The Instruction of Youth* (Gordonville, PA: Gordonville Print Shop, n.d.), 16.

56 *When asked what is the most important thing*: "The Cruelest Kind of Child Abuse," *Family Life*, January 1995, 6.

56 *In her "Tips on Training*: "Tips on Training a Two-Year-Old," *Family Life*, August/September 2009, 11–12.

58 *This favorite schoolroom verse*: *The Instruction of Youth*, 9.

Essay 10. Education: The Way It Should Be

60 *All of that changed abruptly*: See Kraybill, *Riddle of Amish Culture*, rev. ed., 161–87; Kraybill, Johnson-Weiner, and Nolt, *The Amish*, 250–71; Thomas J. Meyers, "Education and Schooling," in *The Amish and the State*, 2nd ed., ed. Donald B. Kraybill (Baltimore: Johns Hopkins University Press, 2003), 87–106.

62 *Finally, in 1972, the court*: Albert N. Keim, ed., *Compulsory Education and the Amish: The Right Not to Be Modern* (Boston: Beacon Press, 1975), 163. See Shawn Francis Peters, *The Yoder Case: Religious Freedom, Education, and Parental Rights* (Lawrence: University Press of Kansas, 2003).

64 *The kind of belonging and well-being*: Hanke Korpershoek, Esther Tamara Canrinus, Marjon Fokkens-Bruinsma, and Hester de Boer, "The Relationships between School Belonging and Students' Motivational, Social-Emotional, Behavioural, and Academic Outcomes in Secondary Education: A Meta-analytic Review," *Research Papers in Education* 35, no. 6 (2020): 641–80, https://www.tandfonline.com/doi/full/10.1080/02671522.2019.1615116.

Essay 11. Apprenticeship: An Old New Idea

69 *What is surprising, however, are headlines*: Scott Carlson, "Why Colleges Need to Embrace the Apprenticeship," *Chronicle of Higher Education*, June 9, 2017, A16–A19.

Essay 12. **Technology: Taming the Beast**

71   *Technology guru Kevin Kelly*: Kevin Kelly, *What Technology Wants* (New York: Penguin Books, 2010).

71   *"Technologically impaired"*: "Weird Al" Yankovic, "Amish Paradise," track 1 on *Bad Hair Day*, Scotti Brothers, 1996. The music video is available on YouTube: https://www.youtube .com/watch?v=lOfZLb33uCg.

72   *Their struggle with motor vehicles*: See Kraybill, *Riddle of Amish Culture*, rev. ed., 213–32; Kraybill, Johnson-Weiner, and Nolt, *The Amish*, 312–34.

Essay 13. **Hacking: Creative Bypasses**

79   *Gid was hacking by creating a workaround*: I am grateful to Kevin Kelly for suggesting in personal conversations that Amish engineers are hackers. He later developed this idea in Kelly, *What Technology Wants*, 217–38.

81   *A couple setting up housekeeping*: The examples of Amishized appliances that follow come from the Amish business maga-zine *Plain Communities Business Exchange* 25, no. 9 (2018).

83   *Horse and progress. That pair of words*: Horse Progress Days, https://horseprogressdays.com/.

Essay 14. **Entrepreneurs: Starting Stuff**

85   *"Entrepreneurs start stuff"*: Wayne Wengerd, "Entrepreneurial Vision," *Plain Communities Business Exchange*, July 2020, 36–39. See Adam Davidson, "An Amish Lesson for Small Busi-ness Success," *Wall Street Journal*, January 18–19, 2020, C5.

85   *Hundreds of microenterprises, from manufacturing*: Donald B. Kraybill and Steven M. Nolt, *Amish Enterprise: From Plows to Profits*, rev. ed. (Baltimore: Johns Hopkins University Press, 2004); Kraybill, Johnson-Weiner, and Nolt, *The Amish*, 291–311.

86   *"Prepping for a party?*: Emma's Popcorn, https://www.emmas popcorn.com/.

88 *Today his booming company*: Pioneer Equipment Inc., https://ackermanequipment.com/pioneer-equipment-inc/.

89 *Several studies report that less than 5 percent*: Donald B. Kraybill, Steven M. Nolt, and Erik J. Wesner, "Sources of Enterprise Success in Amish Communities," *Journal of Enterprising Communities: People and Places in the Global Economy* 5, no. 2 (2011): 112–30.

91 *In his book* Success: Erik J. Wesner, *Success Made Simple: An Inside Look at Why Amish Businesses Thrive* (San Francisco: Jossey-Bass, 2010).

Essay 15. Patience: Slow Down and Listen

93 *An old Amish saying*: Some of the ideas in this essay first appeared in Donald B. Kraybill, "Slow Time Is God's Time: On Patience in the Age of Hypermodernity," Issue Five on Slowness, *Vestoj: The Journal of Sartorial Matters*, no. 5 (2014): 40–48.

94 *Yet we demand more and more*: See Mark C. Taylor, *Speed Limits: Where Time Went and Why We Have So Little Left* (New Haven, CT: Yale University Press, 2014); Mark C. Taylor, "Speed Kills," *Chronicle Review*, October 14, 2014, B6.

94 *The late French scholar Paul Virilio*: See McKenzie Wark, "How Philosopher Paul Virilio (1932–2018) Spoke to an Age of Acceleration and Total War," *Frieze Magazine*, September 19, 2018, https://www.frieze.com/article/how-philosopher-paul virilio-1932-2018-spoke-age-acceleration-and-total-war; Mark Featherstone, "Speed and Violence: Sacrifice in Virilio, Derrida, and Girard," *Anthropoetics: The Journal of Generative Anthropology*, last modified September 17, 2018, http://anthropoetics.ucla.edu/ap0602/virilio/.

Essay 16. Limits: Less Choice, More Joy

100 *Psychologist Barry Schwartz*: Barry Schwartz, *The Paradox of Choice: Why More Is Less* (New York: Harper Perennial,

2004). See Sheena Iyengar, *The Art of Choosing* (New York: Hachette, 2010).

101 *Amish garb illustrates the paradox*: See Kraybill, *Riddle of Amish Culture*, rev. ed., 68–70.

102 *In the larger society, about one in five*: "Should Students Have to Wear School Uniforms?" ProCon, last updated January 20, 2020, https://school-uniforms.procon.org/.

Essay 17. Rituals: A Natural Detox

105 *Nellie Bowles, a* New York Times *reporter*: Nellie Bowles, "How to Feel Nothing Now, in Order to Feel More Later," *New York Times*, November 7, 2019, https://www.nytimes.com/2019/11 /07/style/dopamine-fasting.html?fbclid=IwAR3d2G8Zmw HCKzVmW_U2WaK-RivPx-CbxmYjOHpZs7etrwzkPUZ4 dDKYSMo; Carly Mallenbaum, "What Is Dopamine Fasting and Why Are People Doing It?," *USA Today*, December 5, 2019, https://www.usatoday.com/story/life/2019/12/05 /dopamine-fasting-why-people-avoid-stimulants-name -wellness/4263407002/.

106 *These prayers insert moments of silence*: John A. Hostetler, *Amish Society*, 4th ed. (Baltimore: Johns Hopkins University Press, 1993), 388–90.

108 *An early eighteenth-century devotional booklet*: "Rules of a Godly Life," in *In Meiner Jugend*, 75.

108 *Nature also provides a therapeutic pause*: See Kraybill, Nolt, and Weaver-Zercher, *Amish Way*, 137–50.

109 *One woman described the deep joy*: Katie Troyer, "The Garden Path," *Farming Magazine*, Spring 2002, 44.

Essay 18. Retirement: Aging in Place

111 *In* The Pursuit of Loneliness, *his best-selling 1970 book*: Philip Slater, *The Pursuit of Loneliness* (Boston: Beacon Press, 1970).

111 *Dozens of other authors*: Robert D. Putman, *Bowling Alone*:

The Collapse and Revival of American Community (New York: Simon & Schuster, 2000); Jean M. Twenge and W. Keith Campbell, *The Narcissism Epidemic: Living in the Age of Entitlement* (New York: Simon & Schuster, 2009); Sherry Turkle, *Alone Together: Why We Expect More from Technology and Less from Each Other* (New York: Basic Books, 2011); Vivek H. Murthy, *Together: The Healing Power of Human Connection in a Sometimes Lonely World* (New York: HarperCollins, 2020).

112 *Some twelve million Americans*: "The 'Loneliness Epidemic,'" Health Resources and Services Administration, last reviewed January 2019, https://www.hrsa.gov/enews/past-issues/2019/january-17/loneliness-epidemic; Amy Novotney, "The Risks of Social Isolation: Psychologists Are Studying How to Combat Loneliness in Those Most at Risk, Such as Older Adults," American Psychological Association, May 2019, https://www.apa.org/monitor/2019/05/ce-corner-isolation; Ceylan Yeginsujan, "U.K. Appoints a Minister for Loneliness," *New York Times*, January 18, 2018, https://www.nytimes.com/2018/01/17/world/europe/uk-britain-loneliness.html.

113 *Social isolation and loneliness*: Louis Jacob, Josep Maria Haro, and Ai Koyanagi, "Relationship between Living Alone and Common Mental Disorders in the 1993, 2000 and 2007 National Psychiatric Morbidity Surveys," *PLOS One* 14, no. 5 (2019): e0215182, https://doi.org/10.1371/journal.pone.0215182.

Essay 19. Forgiveness: A Pathway to Healing

117 *There they stood, late one afternoon*: Kraybill, Nolt, and Weaver-Zercher, *Amish Grace*, tells the story of this tragedy.

117 *The English neighbor then turned*: Charlie's wife, Marie, tells her story in Marie Monville and Cindy Lambert, *One Light Still Shines: My Life beyond the Shadow of the Amish Schoolhouse Shooting* (Grand Rapids, MI: Zondervan, 2013).

118 *"We call him our 'angel in black,'"*: Charlie's mother, Terri, tells her story in Terri Roberts and Jeanette Windle, *Forgiven: The Amish School Shooting, A Mother's Love, and a Story of Remarkable Grace* (Bloomington, MN: Bethany House, 2015).

120 *Some pundits proclaimed*: Jeff Jacoby, "Undeserved Forgiveness," *Boston Globe,* October 8, 2006. See also Kraybill, Nolt, and Weaver-Zercher, *Amish Grace*, 56–60.

Essay 20. Suffering: A Higher Plan

125 *The tragedy at Nickel Mines*: Kraybill, Nolt, and Weaver-Zercher, *Amish Grace*, 155–72.

127 *The phrase headlines a collection of stories*: Lyle D. Chupp and JoAnn Chupp, comps., *Thy Will Be Done: 134 Touching Personal Stories of Fatalities among Plain People* (Shipshewana, IN: Lyle and JoAnn Chupp, 1998).

128 *Amish people have always cared for their special-needs children*: See Christian G. Esh, *History of Special Schools and Clinics* (Gordonville, PA: Christian G. Esh, 2017).

129 *In one story, an adult paralyzed by polio*: Shirley Locker, "It's So Daily," *Life's Special Sunbeams*, sample copy 2020, 4.

129 *Now, we call them 'special'"*: Esh, *History of Special Schools and Clinics*, xii.

130 *The story is also remarkable*: Donald B. Kraybill, "Foreword: The Covert Power of Culturalized Medicine," *Our Story in Newsletters, 1989–2018* (Strasburg, PA: Clinic for Special Children, 2019), 6–8.

130 *The cornfield experiment prospered*: Clinic for Special Children, *Annual & Innovation Report*, 2019, https://clinicforspecialchildren.org/wp-content/uploads/2020/03/2019-Annual-Report.pdf.

Essay 21. Nonresistance: No Pushback

133 *It was an aberration of Amish life*: I tell this story in Donald B. Kraybill, *Renegade Amish: Beard Cutting, Hate Crimes, and*

the Trial of the Bergholz Barbers (Baltimore: Johns Hopkins University Press, 2014).

135 *Look at all those pictures and stories*: The full title of *Martyrs Mirror* is *The Bloody Theater, or Martyrs Mirror of the Defenseless Christians, Who Baptized Only upon Confession of Faith, and Who Suffered and Died for the Testimony of Jesus, Their Savior, from the Time of Christ to the Year A.D. 1660*, 2nd English ed., comp. Thieleman J. van Braght (Scottdale, PA: Herald Press, 2002).

136 *If you believe, as the Amish do*: Kraybill, Nolt, and Weaver-Zercher, *Amish Grace*, 167–68.

137 *Nonresistance also guides aspects of daily life*: Hostetler, *Amish Society*, 4th ed., 388–90.

Essay 22. Death: A Good Farewell

139 *Amish funerals are preplanned*: Kraybill, *Riddle of Amish Culture*, rev. ed., 158–60; Kraybill, Johnson-Weiner, and Nolt, *The Amish*, 247–49; Kraybill, Nolt, and Weaver-Zercher, *Amish Way*, 173–78.

141 *In the days after a funeral*: For rituals of grieving, see Kraybill, Nolt, and Weaver-Zercher, *Amish Grace*, 156–60.

143 *Consider, man! The end*: *Unpartheyisches Gesang-Buch: Translations and Lessons*, 2nd ed. (East Earl, PA: Schoolaid, 1997), 171.

Epilogue: Negotiation Never Ends

145 *The riddles of Amish culture:* In the epilogue I focus on technological riddles. Non-technological ones also abound. See Kraybill, *The Riddle of Amish Culture* (1989).

146 *In their view, the solid forms*: Zygmunt Bauman, *Liquid Modernity* (Malden, MA: Blackwell, 2010).

147 *One Amish writer described the melting*: Elmo Stoll, "Why We Live Simply," in *Strangers and Pilgrims* (Aylmer, ON: Pathway, 2003), 8.

148 *The phone has a long and complicated history:* Kraybill, *Riddle of Amish Culture*, rev. ed., 190–97; Diane Zimmerman Umble, *Holding the Line: The Telephone in Old Order Mennonite and Amish Life* (Baltimore: Johns Hopkins University Press, 1996).

153 *That prohibition remains in effect today:* The New Order Amish and several small affiliations permit the use of tractors for working in the fields.

FURTHER READING

Businesses

Kraybill, Donald B., and Steven M. Nolt. *Amish Enterprise: From Plows to Profits*. Rev. ed. Baltimore: Johns Hopkins University Press, 2004.

Wesner, Erik J. *Success Made Simple: An Inside Look at Why Amish Businesses Thrive*. San Francisco: Jossey-Bass, 2010.

Comprehensive Study of Amish Life

Kraybill, Donald B., Karen M. Johnson-Weiner, and Steven M. Nolt. *The Amish*. Baltimore: Johns Hopkins University Press, 2018.

Environment

McConnell, David L., and Marilyn D. Loveless. *Nature and the Environment in Amish Life*. Baltimore: Johns Hopkins University Press, 2018.

Gender and Family

Cates, James A. *Serpent in the Garden: Amish Sexuality in a Changing World*. Baltimore: Johns Hopkins University Press, 2020.

Johnson-Weiner, Karen M. *The Lives of Amish Women*. Baltimore: Johns Hopkins University Press, 2020.

Stevick, Richard A. *Growing Up Amish: The Rumspringa Years*. Rev. ed. Baltimore: Johns Hopkins University Press, 2014.

History

Nolt, Steven M. *A History of the Amish.* 3rd ed. New York: Good Books, 2015.

Language

Louden, Mark L. *Pennsylvania Dutch: The Story of an American Language.* Baltimore: Johns Hopkins University Press, 2015.

Regional Studies

INDIANA

Nolt, Steven M., and Thomas J. Myers. *Plain Diversity: Amish Cultures and Identities.* Baltimore: Johns Hopkins University Press, 2007.

NEW YORK

Johnson-Weiner, Karen M. *New York Amish: Life in the Plain Communities of the Empire State.* 2nd ed. Ithaca, NY: Cornell University Press, 2017.

OHIO

Hurst, Charles E., and David L. McConnell. *An Amish Paradox: Diversity and Change in the World's Largest Amish Community.* Baltimore: Johns Hopkins University Press, 2010.

PENNSYLVANIA

Kraybill, Donald B. *The Riddle of Amish Culture.* Rev. ed. Baltimore: Johns Hopkins University Press, 2001.

Spirituality

Kraybill, Donald B., Steven M. Nolt, and David L. Weaver-Zercher. *Amish Grace: How Forgiveness Transcended Tragedy.* San Francisco: Jossey-Bass, 2007.

Kraybill, Donald B., Steven M. Nolt, and David L. Weaver-Zercher. *The Amish Way: Patient Faith in a Perilous World.* San Francisco: Jossey-Bass, 2010.

Digital Resources

The Amish. Produced by David Belton. Boston: American Experience/ Sarah Colt Productions, 2012. DVD. A 120-minute documentary exploring the beliefs, lifestyle, and history of the Amish as well as their complex relationship to mainstream American culture.

Amish America: https://amishamerica.com/. This blog, developed and run by Erik J. Wesner, is an excellent source of reliable information on Amish topics across America.

Amish Studies: https://groups.etown.edu/amishstudies/. A website with reliable information on Amish life and culture and demographics, developed by the Young Center for Anabaptist and Pietist Studies at Elizabethtown College.

INDEX

About the Author

Donald B. Kraybill is internationally recognized for his scholarship on America's Anabaptist groups. His books, research, and commentary are frequently featured in national and worldwide media. He is a distinguished professor and senior fellow emeritus at the Young Center for Anabaptist and Pietist Studies at Elizabethtown College.

Kraybill is the author, coauthor, or editor of numerous books and articles. His books have been translated into eight different languages. He coauthored the award-winning *Amish Grace: How Forgiveness Transcended Tragedy* as well as *The Amish*—a comprehensive study of Amish life across America. This was a companion book to the two-hour American Experience film (*The Amish*) widely shown on PBS. Other books include his flagship work, *The Riddle of Amish Culture*, and *Renegade Amish*. He coauthored *On the Backroad to Heaven: Old Order Hutterites, Mennonites, Amish, and Brethren*, as well as *The Amish Way: Patient Faith in a Perilous World*.

Besides writing books, Kraybill was the founding editor of Young Center Books in Anabaptist and Pietist Studies, a thirty-volume series published by Johns Hopkins University Press. His groundbreaking research and publications have made a significant contribution to our understanding of some of America's most distinctive ethnic and religious communities.